Volume XVI　　JULY, 1919　　Number 3

Studies in Philology

EDITORIAL COMMITTEE

EDWIN GREENLAW, Managing Editor
WILLIAM M. DEY　　　　GEORGE HOWE

CONTENTS

WITCHCRAFT IN NORTH CAROLINA

By

TOM PEETE CROSS
*Formerly Professor of English in The
University of North Carolina*

485391

Published Quarterly by
THE UNIVERSITY OF NORTH CAROLINA

Yearly Subscription, $2.00—Single Copies, 75 cents

Entered as second-class matter, February 3, 1916, at the post office at Chapel Hill,
North Carolina, under the act of August 24, 1912.

CONTENTS OF VOLUME XV, 1918

	PAGE
E. S. Sheldon. Some English and Old French Phrases	1
William A. Nitze. The Glastonbury Passages in the *Perlesvaus*	7
Walter D. Toy. The Mysticism of Novalis	14
John L. Campion. Das Verwandtschaftsverhältnis der Handschriften des Tristan Ulrichs von Türheim, nebst einer Probe des kritischen Textes	23
J. D. M. Ford. The Teaching of Spanish and our Spanish-American Interests	65
Eden Phillpotts. Hayes Barton	69
Samuel A. Tannenbaum. "Your Napkin is too little; let it alone"	73
Alwin Thaler. Shakespeare's Income	82
Frederick Morgan Padelford. Talus: the Law	97
Edwin Greenlaw. Spenser's Fairy Mythology	105
Robert L. Ramsay. Morality Themes in Milton's Poetry	123
Elbert N. S. Thompson. Milton's "Of Education"	159
James Holly Hanford. The Temptation Motive in Milton	176
Ronald S. Crane. Imitation of Spenser and Milton in the Early Eighteenth Century: A New Document	195
Recent Literature	207
James Holly Hanford and John Marcellus Steadman, Jr. Death and Life: An Alliterative Poem. Edited with Introduction and Notes	221
Donald Clive Stuart. Foreshadowing and Suspense in the Euripidean Prolog	295
Kirby Flower Smith. The Poet Ovid	307
G. A. Harrer. Senatorial Speeches and Letters in Tacitus' *Annals*	332
Charles E. Whitmore. Pindar, *O.* VIII, 53 ff.	344

Studies in Philology

Volume XVI   July, 1919   Number 3

WITCHCRAFT IN NORTH CAROLINA
By Tom Peete Cross

> . . . . ó quam
> Credula mens hominis, et erectae fabulis aures!

The study of popular delusions has far more than an antiquarian or academic interest. Its results constitute one of the most fascinating and instructive chapters in the story of human progress. Written history is not so much the record of battles, conquests, and legislative acts as of social and intellectual development, and no true chronicle of any people can be written until account is taken of its popular beliefs and superstitions, as well as of the more obvious forces that ordinarily engage the attention of the historian. Witch stories are human documents and as such they must be reckoned with in any account of the mental temper of a people who believe in witches and whose actions are, even to a limited extent, ordered in accord with such belief.

With these facts in mind, the branch of the American Folk-Lore Society recently organized in North Carolina has undertaken the task of collecting and recording the popular tradition of that state. The following sketch, prepared at the request of the society, was designed originally to deal with only one of the many phases of folk superstition—Witchcraft; but owing to the heterogeneous character of the collectanea submitted, it has in process of time become a sort of omnium-gatherum of North Carolina tradition regarding magic and supernaturalism. Its purpose is twofold: first, to enumerate such items of witch lore as have already been collected in North Carolina and to point out their traditional character; second, by means of illustrations from the folk-lore of neighboring territory, to indicate what other articles of the diabolical creed future collectors may hope to discover.[1]

Faith in the reality of witchcraft is one of the oldest and most persistent tenets of the human race. Most of us who think at all on the subject doubtless regard the superstition as having originated in that highly developed, complicated, and schematized system for which scholasticism and the Christian church were answerable from the fifteenth to the end of the seventeenth century, but no conclusion could be more erroneous. Witchcraft is as old as history itself, and its existence cannot be laid at the door of the Catholic church or of any other form of religious belief. It "was once universal; it was rooted and grounded in the minds of the people before they became Christians; and it is still the creed of most savages"[2] and of millions of civilized men. The essential principle underlying its manifold composition is *maleficium*, defined by a recent authority as "the working of harm to the bodies and goods of one's fellow-men by means of evil spirits or of strange powers derived from intercourse with such spirits."[3] Before the landing of

---

[1] A small amount of illustrative material of a historical or comparative character has been added, but it is quite from the compiler's purpose to attempt anything like complete documentation except in the case of North Carolina tradition. The curious reader may form an idea of the excessively voluminous literature of witchcraft from such works as Professor George L. Burr's essay on the "Literature of Witchcraft" in the papers of the *American Historical Association* for 1890 (p. 238 ff.). Cf. *Proc. Am. Ant. Soc.*, N. S., XXI (1911), 185 ff., Professor George L. Kittredge's article in the *Proceedings of the American Antiquarian Society*, N. S., vol. XVIII (1907), Wallace Notestein's *History of Witchcraft in England* (Washington, 1911), and Joseph Hansen's *Zauberwahn, Inquisition und Hexenprozess im Mittelalter* (München u. Leipzig, 1900). Cf. W. H. D. Adams, *Witch, Warlock, and Magician*, London, 1889, p. 378 ff. A mass of evidence bearing on the witchcraft superstition in America during the colonial period has been published by Professor Burr in his *Narratives of the Witchcraft Cases* (Original Narratives of Early American History), New York, 1914. Cf. C. W. Upham, *Salem Witchcraft*, Boston, 1867, 2 vols.

[2] Kittredge, *Proc. Am. Ant. Soc.*, XVIII (reprint, p. 4, n. 1). Pertinent observations on the essentially popular character of the witchcraft superstition are to be found in Sir Walter Scott's *Letters on Demonology and Witchcraft*, London, 1830, p. 184 f.

[3] Kittredge, *loc. cit.* Black Magic (designed to cause evil) and White Magic (the purpose of which is to do good) are frequently practiced by the same individual. In North Carolina, as elsewhere, a "witch-doctor" may be also a witch.

the first Europeans on the shores of America, *maleficium* was practiced by the aborigines.[4] It was a powerful force in the lives of the African negroes who came as slaves to these shores.[5] It was also known and feared by the colonists who migrated thither from the British Isles and the continent of Europe.[6] The colonial records

[4] The early settlers of Virginia and North Carolina shared the universal seventeenth-century belief that the Indians, like witches, worshipped the Devil. See John Smith, *The Generall Historie of Virginia*, London, 1624, p. 34. See further *Works of Campain John Smith*, ed., Arber, Birmingham, 1884, pp. 370, 374. John Lawson, in his *History of Carolina*, printed in 1714, states that the Indians of the new country had a god "which is the Devil," and that the old men brought themselves into great esteem "by making others believe their Familiarity with Devils and Spirits" (*History of North Carolina*, a reprint of Lawson's book, Charlotte, 1903, pp. 30, 119). "These people [the Indian conjurers]," says Dr. John Brickell, writing about 1737, "are great Inchanters, and use many Charms of *Witchcraft*," and again, "it is reported by several Planters in those parts, that they raise great Storms of Wind, and that there are many frightful Apparitions that appear above the Fires during the time of their *Conjuration*," the latter accompanied by "a strong smell of *Brimstone*" (*The Natural History of North Carolina*, Dublin, 1737, reprint issued by authority of the Trustees of the Public Libraries, pp. 374, 370). For evidence from New England, see Kittredge, *The Old Farmer and his Almanack*, Boston, 1904, pp. 108 ff., 336, 341.

[5] See, for example, the pertinent remarks of Dr. R. H. Nassau, *Fetichism in West Africa*, New York, 1904, p. 274 ff. Cf. Mary H. Kingsley, *West African Studies*, London, 1899, p. 156 ff.; Sir Harry Johnston, *George Grenfell, and the Congo*, London, I (1908), 35 f., 389 f.

[6] That the colonists brought with them the fundamental doctrines of the witchcraft creed instead of borrowing from the Indians or African slaves or of developing their system independently under the weird influence of their natural surroundings, is easy of demonstration. P. A. Bruce (*Institutional History of Virginia in the Seventeenth Century*, New York and London, I (1910), 280) cites the case of one Captain Bennett, an Englishman engaged in trade with Virginia, who was summoned before the General Court at Jamestown because in 1659 he had hanged at sea an old woman named Katherine Grady who was suspected of witchcraft. On October 5th of the same year Governor Fendall of Maryland, on the complaint of John Washington of Westmoreland County, Virginia, ordered the arrest of Edward Prescott, the charge being that "ye s'd Prescott hanged a witch on his ship as hee was outward bound from England hither, the last yeare." Pending the hearing of the case by the Provincial Court, Prescott gave bond in the sum of 4,000 pounds of tobacco. On being brought to trial, the defendant admitted that a woman named Elizabeth Richardson was hanged on board his ship, but protested that, although he was both merchant and

of Virginia, whose early history is so closely associated with that of North Carolina,[7] contain a number of references to witchcraft among the settlers, and at least one fully developed witch trial— that of Grace Sherwood—took place as late as 1705-6 in Princess Anne County,[8] not far from the border of North Carolina.[9] From

---

owner of the vessel, the captain (John Greene) and the crew threatened to mutiny, when he opposed their action, and that consequently he was forced to permit the hanging. (E. D. Neill, *Virginia Carolorum*, New York, 1886, 256). That the witchcraft prosecutions in New England during the late seventeenth century were the outcome of beliefs imported from the mother country is shown by Kittredge, *Proc. Am. Ant. Soc.*, XVIII, p. 4, n. 1; p. 49, n. 130; *The Old Farmer and his Almanack*, Boston, 1904, p. 110.

[7] See especially *The Writings of "Colonel William Byrd of Westover in Virginia, Esqr.,"* ed., J. S. Bassett, N. Y., 1901, Introdn., p. x f., and Stephen B. Weeks, *Hist. Rev. of the Col. and State Records of North Carolina*, [Raleigh, 1914], p. 4.

[8] From 1637 to 1691 the territory comprised by the present counties of Norfolk and Princess Anne was known as Lower Norfolk County (*Lower Norfolk County, Virginia, Antiquary*, I, 3, n.). For evidence of witchcraft in Lower Norfolk County, see P. A. Bruce, *op. cit.*, I, 279 ff.; Burr, *Narratives*, 435 f.

[9] Grace was the daughter of one John White, a carpenter of Lynnhaven parish, and, at the time of her arraignment, was the widow of James Sherwood, of the same district. At various times from the year of her marriage, 1680, till 1708 Grace figures as plaintiff or defendant in some form of action at law. In 1698 two unsuccessful suits for slander brought by James and Grace Sherwood, show that the latter had been accused by John Gisburne of bewitching his hogs and cotton, and by Anthony Barnes of riding his wife and then escaping "out of the Key hole or crack of the door like a black Catt." In 1705-6 Grace was charged with witchcraft by Luke Hill and wife, against whom she had previously brought action for assault and battery. She was examined by a jury of women and found to have on her body certain marks which indicated that she was a witch. The county court having reached the limit of its authority, the case was referred to the General Court at Williamsburg (Cf. 3 Hening, *Statutes*, 389, Chap. 38), whence, for lack of specific evidence, it was returned to the local authorities. The constable and sheriff were then ordered to search "graces House and all Suspicious places Carfully for all Images and Such like things as may any way Strengthen The Suspicion," but the results are not given. It appears, however, that evidence was forthcoming, and in June, 1706, the county court decided that the plaintiff's guilt "Doth very likely appear." In July, 1706, Grace was bound and "tried in the water by ducking." According to the records, she floated. She was then remanded to jail to await further trial, but, if the matter ever came up again, the records are lost. In any case, she did not die in prison. In 1708 she

these facts it should be obvious that such relics of the witchcraft superstition as exist today in North Carolina are but the result of a belief which has from time immemorial formed part of the intellectual heritage of the human race.

An appreciable effect in preserving among the settlers of Virginia and North Carolina a lively faith in the reality of black magic must be attributed to at least one learned source—Michael Dalton's *Countrey Justice*, an early seventeenth century handbook of legal

---

confessed judgment for a debt due Christopher Cocke. She made her will in 1733, and died before October, 1740, when the document was admitted to probate. A number of local traditions are still associated with her name. Fishermen still point out the Witch-Duck, a spot near the mouth of Lynnhaven Inlet, where Grace is said to have undergone her trial by water. There is a story that, instead of returning to jail, she sailed away to England in an egg-shell, the same sort of vessel in which she had originally come to Virginia. According to another tradition, a millstone which was tied to her when she was placed in the water, floated, and she appeared seated upon it. (During the middle ages saints occasionally travelled on floating stones. *Silva Gadelica*, 1892, II, pp. 11, 33; *Irish Texts Soc.*, XVI (1914), 166.) A poem written by W. A. Swank of Norfolk, attributes to Grace what appears to be a purely fanciful early career in England. For the evidence in the Sherwood case, see *William and Mary College Quarterly Historical Mag.*, 1895; *Lower Norfolk County, Virginia, Antiquary*, II and III; Burr, *op. cit.*, pp. 438 ff. Cf. W. S. Forrest, *Historical and Descriptive Sketches of Norfolk*, Philadelphia, 1853, p. 464; S. G. Drake, *Annals of Witchcraft in New England and Elsewhere in the United States*, Boston, 1869, pp. 210 ff.; O. P. Chitwood, *Johns Hopkins University Studies in History and Political Science*, XXIII, 485, n.; A. M. Gummere, *Witchcraft and Quakerism*, Philadelphia, 1908, p. 37; John Ashton, *The Devil in Britain and America*, London, 1896, p. 313 ff. See further P. A. Bruce, *op. cit.*, I, 278 ff., where evidence on this and other Virginia cases is recorded; and J. C. Wise, *Ye Kingdome of Accawmacke or the Eastern Shore of Virginia in the Seventeenth Century*, Richmond, 1911, p. 47; Burr, *Narratives*, p. 438 ff. Accusations of witchcraft are found in Virginia records as early as 1641. For South Carolina, see Drake, *op. cit.*, p. 215 f.

The ordeal by water, made famous by the seventeenth-century English Witch-Finder General, Matthew Hopkins, is based on the theory that, because of her unclean nature, the witch will not sink in the pure element water, or that, by her connection with Satan, she is rendered preternaturally light. A learned controversy on the subject took place in the eighteenth century between Francis Hutchinson (*An Historical Essay concerning Witchcraft* (1718), London, 1720, ch. XI), and Richard Boulton (*The Possibility and Reality of Magic, Sorcery, and Witchcraft Demonstrated*, etc., London, 1722, ch. VI).

procedure. The book was first printed in 1618 and was often re-edited in Great Britain. It enjoyed wide popularity among the legal profession in the colonies and appears to have been cited as a standard authority during the greater part of the colonial period.[10] In accordance with English law, *The Countrey Justice* declares it a felony " to use or practise Witchcrafts, Enchantment, Charme, or Sorcerie, whereby any person shall be killed, pined, or lamed in any part of their body . . . [or] any cattell or goods shall be destroyed or impaired." "Since," according to the author, "the Justices of peace may not always expect direct evidence," elaborate directions are given for identifying witches, who are pronounced " the most cruell, revengefull, and bloudie " of all sorcerers.[11]

The prominent place occupied by witchcraft in the minds of the colonists is well illustrated by an incidental reference in John Lawson's *History of Carolina*, an early eighteenth-century compendium of information regarding the inhabitants and natural resources of the province, dedicated to the Lords Proprietors, for whom the author acted as surveyor general. It was printed as early as 1709, and the first separate edition appeared in 1714. Apropos of the attitude of the Indians toward spirits, Lawson refers to the many " Hobgoblins and Bugbears as that we [white men] suck in with our milk, and the foolery of our Nurses and Servants suggest to us; who, by their idle Tales of Fairies and Witches, Make impressions on our tender Years, that at Maturity we carry Pigmies' Souls in Giant Bodies and ever after are thereby so much deprived of reason, and Unmann'd, as never to be Masters

---

[10] For references to Dalton's book in catalogues of early Virginia libraries, see *Va. Mag. of Hist. and Biog.*, III, 132; VI, 146; *Wm. and Mary Coll. Qy.*, II, 170; III, 133; VIII, 20, 78. In one case of suspected witchcraft (1675) in Lower Norfolk County (cf. p. 220, n. 8) a jury was ordered " to make deligent search . . . according to the 118 chapter of doulton" (*Wm. and Mary Coll. Qy.*, III, 165). See further *Mass. Records*, II, 212. My colleague, Professor A. P. Scott, to whom I am indebted for these references, assures me that various early Virginia law books quote freely from Dalton.

[11] P. 276 f. of the fifth, revised and enlarged, edition, London, 1635. The British Museum catalogue lists more than half-a-dozen editions of Dalton before the middle of the eighteenth century. A summary of the treatment of witchcraft found in the 1655 edition is given by E. L. Linton, *Witch Stories*, London, 1861, p. 182, n.

of half the Bravery Nature designed for us."[12] These words, with a few trivial alterations, are repeated in *The Natural History of North Carolina*, published in 1737 by one Dr. John Brickell,[13] a physician who is said to have practiced in Edenton about 1730.

The following passage is found in Dr. Joseph Doddrige's *Notes on the Settlement and Indian Wars of the Western Parts of Virginia & Pennsylvania, from the Year 1763 until the Year 1783, Inclusive, Together with a View of the State of Society and Manners of the First Settlers of the Western Country* (Wellesburgh, Va., 1824, p. 161 ff.).[13a] It was later incorporated by Mann Butler, an early historian of Kentucky, in his more extensive description of the "Manners and Habits of the Western Pioneers," written about 1836 (MS. *Durrett D 3333*, p. 56 ff.: University of Chicago Library) whence for convenience the present transcript is taken. The data were gathered in northwestern Virginia (near the Kentucky border), but, as Butler observes, the account may be taken as 'a faithful picture of early frontier conditions throughout

---

[12] *The History of Carolina*, by John Lawson, Gent., London, 1714, reprinted as *History of North Carolina*, Charlotte, 1903. The passage quoted is found on page 118 of the reprint. Lawson may be repeating an old theory rather than speaking from personal observation or experience. John Webster, in his famous *Displaying of Supposed Witchcraft*, written in 1677, blames idle tales heard in youth for much of the belief in witchcraft in his day. ((See p. 32 of the first edition.) For an account of the editions of Lawson's *History*, see Weeks, *An. Rep. Am. Hist. Assn.*, 1895, p. 230 f.

[13] *The Natural History of North Carolina*, by John Brickell, M. D., Dublin, 1737 (Reprint, p. 354). Brickell appropriates almost verbatim and without acknowledgment not only this but many other passages in Lawson's *History*. Attention was called to the plagiarism in the *No. Am. Rev.*, XXIII (N. S. XIV), 1826, p. 288, note, but, as Weeks shows (*An. Rep. Am. Hist. Assn.*, 1895, p. 234), Brickell's work is "a good deal more than a mere slavish reprint of Lawson."

[13a] In the copy before me the title-page is lacking. According to Sabin a second edition appeared at Winchester in 1833. Another edition, by Alfred Williams, "with a Memoir of the Author by his Daughter," appeared at Albany in 1876, and parts of the book have been printed several times, but the complete early editions are said to be extremely rare. As the text of the manuscript was in type before I discovered a copy of Dr. Doddridge's book and as the differences between the two are unimportant, I have allowed the former to stand.

the western country generally,' including, of course, the highlands of Carolina.

"The belief in witchcraft," writes Dr. Doddridge, "was prevalent among the settlers of the western country. To the witch was ascribed the tremendous power of inflicting strange and incurable diseases, particularly on children, of destroying cattle by shooting them with hair-balls, and a great variety of other means of destruction; of inflicting spells and curses on guns and other things, and lastly, of changing men into horses, and after bridling and saddling, riding them in full speed over hill and dale to their frolics and other places of rendezvous. Wizards were men supposed to possess the same mischievous powers as the witches; but they were seldom exercised for bad purposes. The powers of wizards were exercised for the purpose of counteracting the malevolent influences of the witches of the other sex. I have known several of these witchmasters, as they were called, who made a public profession of curing the diseases inflicted by the influence of witches; and I have known respectable physicians, who had no greater portion of business, in the line of their profession, than many of these witch-masters had in theirs. . . . Diseases which could not be accounted for nor cured, were usually ascribed to some supernatural agency of a malignant kind. For the cure of the diseases inflicted by witchcraft, the picture of the supposed witch was drawn on a stump or piece of board, and shot at with a bullet containing a little bit of silver. This silver bullet transferred a painful and sometimes a mortal spell on that part of the witch corresponding with the part of the portrait struck by the bullet. The witch had but one way of relieving herself from any spell inflicted on her in this way, which was that of borrowing something, no matter what, of the family to which the subject of the exercise of her witch-craft belonged. I have known several poor old women much surprised at being refused requests which had been usually granted without hesitation, and almost heart-broke when informed of the cause of the refusal. When cattle or hogs were supposed to be under the influence of witchcraft, they were burnt in the forehead by a branding iron, or when dead, burned wholly to ashes. This inflicts a spell upon the witch, that could only be removed by borrowing, as above stated. Witches were often said to milk the cows of their neighbors. This they did by fixing a new pin in a towel for each cow intended to be milked. This towel was hung over her own door, and by means of certain incantations, the milk was extracted from the fringes of the towel, after the manner of milking a cow. This happened when the cows were too poor to give much milk."

R. G. Thwaites, who had at his disposal the valuable Draper manuscript materials on early frontier history, is authority for the assertion that during the latter half of the eighteenth century the inhabitants of Davie County, North Carolina, " firmly believed in the existence of witches " and that " bad dreams, eclipses of the sun, the howling of dogs and the croaking of ravens" were sure prologues to coming disaster.[14]

Testimony of a more satisfactory character is furnished by the autobiography of Rev. Brantley York, who was born in 1805. York states that during the early nineteenth century the inhabitants of the Bush Creek district in Randolph County, where he spent part of his boyhood, "believed in Witchcraft, Ghost-seeing, haunted houses and fortune telling." "When the neighbors came together," he continues, "the most prominent topic of conversation was relating some remarkable witch tales, ghost stories and conjurations of various kinds; and so interesting was (sic) these stories that the conversation often continued until a very late hour at night. Often have I sat and listened to these stories till it seemed to me that each hair upon my head resembled the quill of a porcupine. I was afraid to go out of doors, afraid to go to bed alone, and almost afraid of my own shadow."[15] A striking instance of the influence exerted by witchcraft on the country people of western North Carolina at a somewhat later date is furnished by Mr. Charles L. Coon, of Wilson, to whom the writer is indebted for the use of his collectanea. The events occurred during the second quarter of the last century in "an isolated section of Lincoln County originally settled by Germans and a few English." The account as given by Mr. Coon is as follows:

"My father, who was born in 1834, has often told me that one of his earliest recollections centered around the death of a young neighbor boy who received no other medical attention to aid him in combatting a severe

---

[14] R. G. Thwaites, *Daniel Boone*, New York, 1902, p. 32.

[15] *The Autobiography of Brantley York* (John Lawson Monographs of the Trinity College Historical Society, 1), Durham, 1910, p. 8 f. Of conditions during the early nineteenth century in Bedford County, Virginia, Dr. J. B. Jeter (born 1802) writes: "Story-telling was one of the common amusements of the times; and these stories usually related to witches, hags, giants, prophetic dreams, ghosts and the like. The dread of jack-o'-lanterns, graveyards and ghosts was quite common, and extended much beyond the avowed belief in their reality. Haunted spots were quite common, to which timid passengers usually gave a wide berth in the night. Ghosts were not unfrequently seen gliding about in the twilight, or in the moonshine, clothed in white." He then tells the story of how he himself once came near seeing a ghost. For the whole passage, see Wm. E. Hatcher, *Life of J. B. Jeter, D. D.*, Baltimore, 1887, p. 36 f. I am indebted to my colleague, Professor Wm. E. Dodd, for calling my attention to this book.

case of typhoid fever than that supplied by the neighboring witch doctor. This boy's parents were ignorant and superstitious, and believed in witches and in the powers witches were supposed to possess. When their young son fell sick, they imagined he had been bewitched; so the doctor was sent for. He came and told the parents that their surmisings were correct, that witches had certainly caused the sickness of their child. Confidingly the parents permitted the witch doctor to have his way, and the treatment for 'witches' was immediately begun. First, the 'doctor' ordered the return of all borrowed property to the owners and also ordered that the parents of the sick boy call in everything which happened to have been borrowed from them. These orders embraced everything, and one neighbor was very much inconvenienced by having to return a log-chain which he was using and could not at the time replace without purchasing a new one. But finally all borrowed property was in place, and then the doctor proceeded to treat the bewitched boy. For several weeks he visited the patient and put him through many physical calisthenics, all the while uttering in a low voice what appeared to be magic words or incantations in Pennsylvania Dutch to drive away the spell wrought by the witches. But no one understood or could interpret the magic words which were used. Days passed and the child finally died. The witch doctor then reluctantly admitted that the spell of the witches was beyond his power. The death of this young child under such circumstances seems not to have caused any great public indignation at the time. Only upon a few persons in the neighborhood did this death make any lasting impression, so general was the belief in witches."

Judge G. A. Shuford told Mr. J. P. Arthur of a reputed witch known as "Granny" Weiss or Weice, who lived on the French Broad River, near the mouth of Davidson's River, about a century ago. On being consulted by a man named Johnson who was suffering from gravel, she informed the patient that unless he returned several hundred dollars which, as she happened to know, he had stolen from a cattle buyer, he could not be cured. Johnson accordingly restored the money, but whether he was healed of his ailment is not told. In any case, the story of the theft got abroad, and he was forced to leave the neighborhood.[16]

As will appear from the following pages, a considerable body of testimony is available for the study of the witchcraft superstition in North Carolina during the last half century.

Although in North Carolina the term witch, true to its historical usage, is still applied to either sex, now, as of yore, more women than men are accused of dabbling in the black art.[17] The following

[16] J. P. Arthur, *Western North Carolina*, Raleigh, 1914, p. 342.
[17] King James I. was merely repeating an older tradition when, in his

account, furnished by Mr. G. T. Stephenson, formerly of Pendleton, North Carolina, concerns a woman who was reputed to be a witch.[18]

"The early years of Phœbe Ward, witch, are shrouded in mystery. It is known that she was a woman of bad morals. No one seemed to know anything of her past. She was an old, old woman when this account begins.

"Phœbe Ward had no fixed home. She lived here and there, first at one place and then at another in Northampton County, North Carolina. She stayed in a hut or any shelter whatsoever that was granted her.

"She made her living by begging from place to place. Most people were afraid to refuse her, lest she should apply her witchcraft to them. When she found a house at which people were particularly kind to her, there she stopped and abused their kindness. Hence the people resorted to a number of methods to keep her away. For instance, when they saw her coming, they would stick pins point-up into the chair-bottoms, and then offer her one of these chairs. It is said that she could always tell when the chair was thus fixed, and would never sit in it. Also, they would throw red pepper into the fire, and Phœbe would leave as soon as she smelled it burning. . . .

"Among her arts it is said that she could ride persons at night (the same as nightmares), that she could ride horses at night, and that when the mane was tangled in the morning it was because the witch had made stirrups of the plaits. She was said to be able to go through key-holes, and to be able to make a horse jump across a river as if it were a ditch. She was credited with possessing a sort of grease which she could apply, and then slip out of her skin and go out on her night rambles, and on her return get back again. It is said that once she was making a little bull jump across the river, and as she said, 'Through thick, through thin; 'way over in the hagerleen,' the animal rose and started. When he was about half way over, she said, 'That was a damn'd good jump,' and down the bull came into the river. (The witch is not to speak while she is crossing.)[19]

---

famous treatise on *Daemonologie* (1597), he asserted that during the sixteenth century female witches were largely in the majority (See p. 116 of the 1616 edn.). See further Reginald Scot, *The Discoverie of Witchcraft* (1584), ed., B. Nicholson, London, 1886, p. 93. Cf. Jules Bois, *Le Satanisme et la Magie*, Paris, 1895, especially Chap. II.

[18] As printed, *Journal of American Folk-Lore*, XXII (1909), 252 f. The version here given is the source of Miss Elizabeth A. Lay's drama, "When Witches Ride," printed in the University of North Carolina *Magazine*, April, 1919.

[19] In an Irish folk-tale recorded by B. Hunt (*Folk Tales of Breffny*, Macmillan, 1912, p. 11), an old man mounted on a yearling calf, rides out one night with a band of fairy-folk, or "good people." "It wasn't long before they came to a big lake that had an island in the middle of it. With one spring the whole party landed on the island and with another

"To keep the witch away people nailed horse-shoes with the toe up over the stable-doors. To keep her from riding persons at night, they hung up sieves over the door. The witch would have to go through all the meshes before she could enter, and by the time she could get through, it would be day, and she would be caught.

"Phœbe came near meeting a tragic death before her allotted time was out. One night several men of the neighborhood gathered around a brandy-barrel. As the liquor flowed, their spirits rose, and they were on the lookout for some fun. They went over to where Phœbe was staying and found her asleep. Thinking she was dead, they shrouded her, and proceeded to hold the wake. They were soon back at their demijohns, and while they were standing in one corner of the room drinking, there came a cracked, weak voice from the other corner, where the supposed corpse was lying out, 'Give me a little; it's mighty cold out here.' They all fled but one,— Uncle Bennie,—and he was too drunk to move. When things became quiet and Phœbe repeated her request, he said, 'Hush, you damn'd b—h, I'm goin' to bury you in the mornin'.' The others were afraid to return that night, but did so the next morning, and found Bennie and Phœbe sitting before the fire, contented, warm, and drinking brandy.

"After this Phœbe lived several years, making her livelihood by begging. Her last days were as mysterious as her early life had been."

Like her kinswomen of the past, the modern female witch, though generally old, is not always so. A batch of witch lore received in 1908 from an old negro woman in southeastern Virginia contains the information that the black art is sometimes practiced by young girls. That the ancient principle, *si saga sit mater, sic etiam est filia,* still holds good, is illustrated by an account of the daughter of a North Carolina witch, who, while accompanying her mother on one of her midnight rambles, got into serious trouble.[20] The witch of today is also like her ancestors in having certain physical peculiarities which differentiate her

they were safe on the far shore. 'Damn, but that was a great lep for a yearling calf,' said Paddy. With that one of the Good People struck him a blow on the head, the way the sense was knocked out of him and he fell on the field."

[20] For the story, see *J. A. F.-L.,* XXII (1909), 251. In connection with the trial of witches at Lancaster, England, in 1612, a girl of fourteen confessed that one night she had been carried by her grandmother and aunt (two witches) to the house of one Thomas Walshman (Thomas Wright, *Narratives of Sorcery and Magic,* London, 1851, II, 129; cf. 140). Cf. Burr, *Narratives,* 345. Children, as well as adults, were formerly executed for witchcraft. See A. F. Chamberlain, *The Child and Childhood in Folk Thought,* N. Y., 1896, 323.

from the common run of womankind. According to the old negro just referred to, a witch's breasts are situated under her arms, and the skin about her neck resembles a collar.[21] The witch of the seventeenth century also bore on her body certain marks or teats which were the seal of her compact with Satan [22] or were sucked by her familiar demons and which were often used by courts of justice as means of identification.[23] Reginald Scot, who deserves high honor for having raised his voice against the well nigh universal belief in witchcraft during the sixteenth century, asserts that in his day (his famous *Discoverie of Witchcraft* was published in 1584), a suspected witch who had " anie privie marke under her arm pokes" was regarded by the courts as guilty.[24] The following is according to Dalton: "Their [witches'] . . . familiar hath some big or little teat upon their body, & in some secret place, where hee sucketh them. And besides their sucking, the Devil leaveth other marks upon their body, sometimes like a blew spot, or red spot, like a Flea-biting . . . And these the Devills markes be insensible, & being pricked will not bleed, & be often in their secretest parts, and therefore require diligent and carefull search."[25] As lately as 1706 Grace Sherwood, on trial for witchcraft before the court of Princess Anne County, Virginia, was examined by a jury of women and found to have " two things like titts on her private parts of a Black Coller, being Blacker than the Rest of her Body." According to the old woman who furnished the information about the witch-marks, a male witch will not look you in the

---

[21] Cf. *J. A. F.-L.*, XXII, 251.

[22] An old song, said to have been current for more than a hundred years in central North Carolina, refers to the sign placed by the Devil on the forehead of those "that he claims for his own." Mrs. E. M. Backus, the *collect*or, says, "I have heard before of the two marks of Satan, one in the head and one in the hand, I believe, of this shape ∓ " (*J. A. F.-L.*, XIV (1901), 291). The mark by which the devil brands witches is referred to in a seventeenth century pamphlet of instructions to jurymen (See below, p. 230, n. 26).

[23] See Notestein, *op. cit.*, pp. 36, 155. Cf. King James I, *Daemonologie*, 1616 edn., p. 105; Matthew Hopkins, *Discovery of Witches*, 1647, 3 f.; Joseph Glanvill, *Sadducismus Triumphatus* (on which see below, p. 230, n. 27), 4th edn., London, 1726, pp. 295, 298 f.; S. G. Drake, *op. cit.*, 80 f.; Burr, *Narratives*, pp. 344, 436, n. 1.

[24] *Op. cit.*, 21.

[25] *Op. cit.*, p. 277.

face, a habit which, Scot asserts,[26] was attributed to all witches in the sixteenth century.

In North Carolina, where, as in other Christian communities, the Devil is ever ready to deceive the unwary, license to practice witchcraft is often received directly from his Satanic Majesty, who in exchange takes a mortgage on the soul of the pupil as he did on that of Doctor Faustus hundreds of years ago.[27] The story told

[26] *Op. cit.*, pp. 16, 20. According to sixteenth-century opinion a witch cannot weep (Scot, *op. cit.*, p. 22). The tests applied to witches by seventeenth-century English courts are given by Robert Filmer in *An Advertisement to the Jury-Men of England touching Witches* (1652), London, 1680, p. 304 ff. Cf. Burr, *Narratives*, p. 304, n. 5.

[27] The articles of the demon contract are discussed along with a detailed exposition of the whole science of black magic in the *Malleus Maleficarum*, or "Witch-Hammer" (published in 1489), perhaps the most famous handbook of witchcraft ever written. See the 1620 (London) edition, I, 27, 148, 160; II, Part II, 37, 372, 382. Cf. A. M. Pratt, *The Attitude of the Catholic Church toward Witchcraft*, etc., Washington (D. C.), 1915, p. 57. Various phases of the witchcraft superstition are seriously discussed from the standpoint of seventeenth-century metaphysics and natural philosophy by that famous enemy of the Devil and his earthy servants, Joseph Glanvill, Fellow of the Royal Society and Chaplain in Ordinary to His Majesty King Charles II., in a tract entitled *Some Philosophical Considerations Touching the Being of Witches and Witchcraft* (1666). See pp. 15 ff. of the second edition, London, 1667. Glanvill's arguments for the existence of witches are repeated in *A Blow at Modern Sadducism in Some Philosophical Considerations about Witchcraft* (See pp. 15 ff. of the fourth edition, corrected and enlarged, London, 1668), and are set forth more fully in his still well-known *Sadducismus Triumphatus: A Full and Plain Evidence concerning Witches and Apparitions*, first published in 1681 (See pp. 6 ff. of the fourth [1726] edition). On Glanvill's importance in the history of English witchcraft, see Kittredge, *Proc. Am. Ant. Soc.*, XVIII, 13. Glanvill's attempt to prove scientifically the reality of the demon contract, animal transformation, and other tenets of the witchcraft creed, was answered by John Webster in *The Displaying of Supposed Witchcraft*, London, 1677. See further Alexander Roberts, *A treatise on Witchcraft*, London, 1616, p. 28 ff.; John Wagstaffe, *The Question of Witchcraft Debated*, 2d edn., London, 1671, p. 101 ff. Cf. Paul Carus, *History of the Devil and the Idea of Evil*, Chicago, 1900, p. 414 ff. For other early evidence, see Wright, *Narratives*, II, pp. 88, 96, 114 f., 151, 153; *Daemonologia: A Discourse on Witchcraft as it was Acted in the Family of Mr. Edward Fairfax, of Fuyston, in the County of York, in the Year 1621*, ed., W. Grainge, Harrogate, 1882, pp. 40 ff. Cf. Scot, *op. cit.*, pp. 31 ff.; Grimm, *Deut. Mythol.*, 4th edn., Berlin, 1876, II, 894 f.; Karl Knortz, *Streifzüge auf dem Gebiete amerikanischer Volkskunde*, Leipzig, 1902, pp. 130 ff.; Ashton, *op. cit.*, pp. 148 ff.

below was related to Mr. Thomas Smith, of Zionville, North Carolina, by Sam Guy, an uneducated man of some sixty-five years, who has spent most of his life in the mountains. Sam is known as a successful squirrel hunter and a great digger of 'sang' (ginseng). He is a firm believer in witchcraft and can justify his faith by a large number of authentic cases, of which the following is a sample:

"Ye know Eph Tucker that used to live on the Hashion? Well, he wuz all'us counted a mighty truthful man, and he used to tell me a sight o' tales about witches. He said when he lived down in Ashe, there was a man named Ferro who shore could bewitch people. . . . One day [Eph.] says to Ferro, says he, 'I want to learn to bewitch folks like you can.' Ferro kindly agreed to show him how to be a witch. He says, 'You come with me out in the road.' They went out in the wagin road, and Ferro tuck a stick and made a ring in the dirt. 'Now you git in that ring,' says Ferro. Eph, he got in the ring. 'Now squat down,' says Ferro. Eph, he squatted down. 'Now,' says Ferro, 'put one hand under yer right foot and tother hand on top o' yer head.'[28] Well, Eph put one hand under his foot and tother on top o' his head. 'Now,' says Ferro, 'you say ater me: "Devil take me, ring and all."'. Eph said he wuz a-gittin' a little bit skeered by this time, but he said what ole Ferro told him—'Devil take me, ring and all'—and about that time the ground begin to sink right under him. Eph says he felt himself a-goin' right down. He shore was skeered by this time, and he give a jump right out o' the ring and run from that place as hard as he could."[29] He didn't turn his head to look back. Ater that Eph said he never tried to be a witch any more."

Judged by the following passage from Dalton, old Ferro's instructions combine the practice of witchcraft with that of conjury, between which the legal authority is careful to distinguish. Whereas the witch deals with the Devil "rather by a friendly and voluntarie conference or agreement between him (or her) and the devill or familiar," conjurers "beleeve by certain terrible words, that they can raise the Devill, and make him to tremble; and by impailing themselves in a circle (which as one saith, cannot keep

---

[28] In 1678 Annabil Stuart, tried for witchcraft at Paisley, Scotland, confessed that as part of the ceremony of giving herself to the Devil, "she put her hand to the crown of her head, and the other to the sole of her foot." Glanvill, op. cit., p. 391.

[29] On the circle as a protection against the powers of evil, see F. D. Bergen, *Animal and Plant Lore Collected from the Oral Tradition of English Speaking People*, Boston and N. Y., 1899, p. 13.

out a mouse) they beleeve that they are therein insconsed, and safe from the Devill whom they are about to raise." [30]

Among the mountain whites of the southern Alleghanies it was possible some twenty years since for a man to acquire forbidden knowledge by "scouring a tin or pewter plate in some secret place, and giving himself to the Devil by saying, 'I will be as clean of Jesus Christ as this dish is of dirt.'" [31] In Knott County, Kentucky, said to have been settled by emigrants from Virginia and North Carolina, a woman may become a witch by taking a handkerchief and gun, ascending the highest neighboring mountain before sunrise, and proceeding as follows: "Just as the fiery ball appears above the eastern horizon, with uttered imprecations against Deity and prayers to the Devil, she is to shoot a bullet through the handkerchief as she holds it up toward the rising sun. If blood flows from the torn cloth, she is an accepted member of the witches' crew." [32] The ratification of the compact, here shown by the bleeding of the handkerchief, is generally indicated by other means. The method of procedure adopted in the following account from Scott County, east Tennessee, has the sanction of a long line of tradition. The narrator, an old white man, said that on one occasion he had stolen and used some white powder which formed part of the stock in trade of a witch. Later he met "a very small, dark-haired, red-complected man" who said, "You have used some of my material, and now you must put your name in my book." The trembling mortal wrote his name with his own blood in the stranger's book, but he must have desisted from using the diabolical stuff, for the Devil never came to claim his victim. [33]

The examination of Elizabeth Style, of Stoke Trister, Somerset, before an English justice in 1664, shows that the ceremony

---

[30] *Op. cit.*, p. 279.

[31] J. A. Porter, "Folk-Lore of the Mountain Whites of the Alleghanies," *J. A. F.-L.*, VII (1894), 107.

[32] H. G. Shearin, "Some Superstitions of the Cumberland Mountains," *J. A. F.-L.*, XXIV (1911), 320. Cf. Notestein, *op. cit.*, p. 153.

[33] *J. A. F.-L.*, XIII (1900), 210. Compare the story of the little girl and the Devil in "Negro Folk Lore and Witchcraft in the South," *J. A. F.-L.*, III (1890), 203. It would be surprising if the tale of "The Devil and Tom Walker," known elsewhere in the United States, is not preserved in North Carolina. Cf. Karl Knortz, *Streifzüge auf dem Gebiete amerikanischer Volkskunde*, p. 130 f.

described above finds good authority in seventeenth century practice. The defendant confessed that the Devil had appeared to her "in the shape of a handsome Man, and after of a black Dog," and had offered her wealth and happiness for twelve years if she would "sign his Paper," observe his laws, and let him suck her blood. When she agreed, "he prick'd the fourth Finger of her Right-hand, between the middle and upper Joint, (where the sign at the Examination remained) and with a Drop or two of her Blood, she signed the Paper with an [O]. Upon this, the Devil gave her Sixpence, and vanish'd with the paper." [34]

The modern American witch, though perhaps not quite so malignant as her predecessors, is fully equipped with a wide range of uncanny powers. Like the witches of all time, she is a shape-shifter of astonishing versatility. According to Rev. Brantley York,[35] the inhabitants of Randolph County, North Carolina, a century ago believed that witches could transform themselves into any variety of bird or beast, but it is probable that then as now North Carolina witches assumed by preference the form of special animals.[36]

From ancient times the cat has been regarded as endowed with supernatural qualities,[37] and has been associated with practitioners of the black art. To kill a cat is everywhere bad luck.[38] It is also

[34] Glanvill, op. cit., p. 295. Frequently the Devil's wages turn out to be worthless, as in a negro story from Guilford County, North Carolina. The Devil gave a fiddler fifty cents for playing two tunes, but the man, on reaching home, discovered that he had nothing in his pocket but filth (J. A. F.-L., xxx [1917], 180).

[35] Autobiog., p. 8.

[36] The following comes from Guilford County. A farmer who was at enmity with one of his neighbors discovered that a large white horse was destroying his tobacco. "So he made up his mind to stop it that night. He went to de fence an' gathered him up a rail, an' sot down. An' when de horse come, an' at full speed, he knocked it backuds with the rail. It was that other man's wife he foun' layin' over the other side of the fence a-shiverin'."—Negro. (J. A. F.-L., xxx (1917), 186.)

[37] On demon cats, see [Harvard] Studies & Notes in Philol. and Lit., VIII (1903), 259, n. 2; Grimm, Deut. Mythol., 4th edn., Berlin, 1876, II, 873. On animal demons, see M. D. Conway, Demonology and Devil-Lore, 3d edn., New York, 1889, I, 121 ff. Cf. A. Wuttke, Der deutsche Volksaberglaube der Gegenwart (3d edn., by E. H. Meyer), Berlin, 1900, p. 151.

[38] For evidence from the mountains of North Carolina, see J. A. F.-L., xx (1907), 245.

unlucky to sleep with [39] or even cross the path of a cat.[40] Cats suck the breath of sleeping infants [41] and sometimes mutilate corpses.[42] It is good luck for a cat to come to the house,[43] but in North Carolina, when a family moves, the cat should never be taken.[44] Tails, skins, and bones of black cats are widely used both in witchcraft and in popular preventive medicine.[45] During the great flourishing period of European witchcraft the cat often served as a disguise for the witch's familiar and even for the hag herself.[46] Today North Carolina witches often appear in the form of cats, and with the worst witches known to the mountain whites of the Alleghanies lycanthropy is common.[47] In a story told by a negress in Baltimore, Maryland, two white ladies of apparently irreproachable life who were wont to slip out of their skins and sally forth nightly and who were not cured of their shape-shifting propensities until salt was rubbed on their raw hides, always assumed the form of cats before scampering up the chimney.[48] Cats as familiars of

[39] *J. A. F.-L.*, XII (1899), 268 (Ga.).

[40] *Southern Workman and Hampton School Quarterly*, XLI (1913), 246. See further p. 235, n. 49, below.

[41] *J. A. F.-L.*, XII (1899), 268 (Ga.).

[42] F. D. Bergen, *Animal and Plant Lore*, p. 81. Cf. E. H. Meyer, *Badisches Volksleben*, Strassburg, 1900, p. 584.

[43] *J. A. F.-L.*, XI (1898), 12 (Md.).

[44] *J. A. F.-L.*, XX (1907), 244. Among the Cumberland Mountains it is good luck to find a cat of three colors, and, as long as you keep one, the house will not burn down (E. B. Miles, *The Spirit of the Mountains*, N. Y., 1905, p. 104).

[45] *J. A. F.-L.*, XV (1902), 191 (Washington, D. C.); XXII (1909), 255; F. D. Bergen, *Animal and Plant Lore*, p. 71. Cf. *J. A. F.-L.*, XI (1898), 12; W. G. Black, *Folk-Medicine* (Publns. of the Folk-Lore Soc., XII), L., 1883, p. 151.

[46] "These Witches have ordinarily a familiar spirit, which appeareth to them; sometimes in one shape, sometimes in another; as in the shape of a Man, Woman, Boy, Dogge, Cat, Foale, Fowle, Hare, Rat, Toad, &c. And to these their spirits they give names, and they meete together to christen them." Dalton, *op. cit.*, p. 277. See further Notestein, *op. cit.*, pp. 35, 327; Scot, *op. cit.*, p. 8; Glanvill, *Sad. Triumph.*, pp. 298, 334, 398.

[47] *J. A. F.-L.*, VII (1894), 114 f. Cf. Harvard *Studies & Notes*, VIII (1903), 169, n. 1, 260 ff.; Sir Walter Scott, *Letters on Demonology and Witchcraft*, p. 211 ff.; John Webster, *Displaying of Supposed Witchcraft*, edn. cit., pp. 33, 91; Reginald Scot, *op. cit.*, p. 71.

[48] *J. A. F.-L.*, XII (1899), 145 f. Scot (*op. cit.*, p. 73) cites the case of three witches who transformed themselves into cats to bedevil a faggot-

witches figure in Harrison Ainsworth's *Lancashire Witches* and in Miss Mary Johnston's *Witch;* and stories of the same general type as Joel Chandler Harris's well-known "Plantation Witch" frequently represent the "hant" as appearing in the form of a cat.[49] The following tale from Northampton County, of which a Guilford County version has already been published,[50] is furnished by Mr. G. T. Stephenson:

"An old house was haunted and nobody would stay in it. At last a foolhardy negro, under a wager, undertook to spend the night in the house. Soon after he had put the light out and gone to bed he saw sitting on the foot of the bed a big black cat with eyes that looked like moons, licking his whiskers. The cat mewed, 'There ain't nobody here but you and me, is there?' The negro rose up and said, 'Naw, and there ain't gwine to be nobody here but you long.' And with that he went out the window, taking the window-sash with him, and down the road like a streak of lightning. Having run out of breath the negro sat down on a log beside the road to rest. Looking up and towards the other end of the log he saw the same black cat sitting there. And the cat mewed, 'That was a right good race we had.' With that, the negro said, 'Dat ain't nothin' to what we's gwine to have,' and lit out again. The next morning those who had made the wager went to the haunted house to see what had happened and found the window-sash gone and no signs of the negro. Two or three days afterwards the negro came straggling in all bedraggled and with his clothes half torn off him. One of them asked him where he had been the last two or three days and he answered, 'I've been comin' back.'"[51]

---

maker. Their victim, "having hurt them all with a faggot sticke, was like to have been put to death."

[49] The witch's familiar, when a cat, is generally black, and all cats of that color are more or less possessed. Nevertheless, when a witch assumes the form of a cat, the animal is not necessarily black. See *J. A. F.-L.*, IV (1891), 324; VIII (1895), 252 (S. C.); X (1897), 76; XII (1899), 145 (Md.); XIII (1900), 227 (Ga., negro). Among the negroes of tidewater Georgia and South Carolina witches derive their power from the possession of a particular bone from the body of a black cat (*So. Workman*, XXXIV [1905], 634 f.; *J. A. F.-L.*, XXVII [1914], 247). In the mountains of North Carolina, "if a cat sits down among a crowd of girls, the one she looks at will marry first" (*J. A. F.-L.*, XX (1907), 245). The Chicago *American* for May 8, 1915, records the case of an English maidservant who hesitated to sail on the ill-fated "Lusitania" because she had seen a black cat before going aboard. Late in the sixteenth century certain Scottish witches caused a terrible storm at sea by throwing a cat into the water (*Newes from Scotland*, etc., 1591 [Roxburghe Club, 1816]).

[50] *J. A. F.-L.*, XXX, 195.

[51] During the writer's boyhood another version of this story was widely known throughout eastern Virginia and North Carolina through the telling of the popular entertainer, Polk Miller.

The demon cat in Mr. Stephenson's story may not have been a transmogrified witch, but the case is perfectly clear in the following negro story from Guilford County, North Carolina, which represents one of the multitudinous forms of the well-nigh worldwide motif of the defence of a house against a haunting goblin. The theme is embodied in the famous account of Beówolf's fight with Grendel in Hrothgar's hall, and Harris has an interesting variant in his *Daddy Jake the Runaway*.

"Der was a man owned a mill, an' he couldn't stay at it late. Something would run him away. One day an ol' traveller (var., preacher) came along, an' asked him what would he give him to stay dere dat night. He said he would give him mos' anything if he would stay. So he went in, an' takin' (leg. taken?) his book, his Bible, an' surd, an' sat down an' kimminced a-readin'. It was eight or nine cats came in 'rectly after dark, an' staid there until gettin' late. An' one of them made a drive at de man, an' he up with his surd an' cut his right front foot off. An' dey all left then. Nex' mornin' he went up to de house fur breakfast. An' de miller he was gettin' breafas'. His wife was not able. He wanted to know what was de trouble. He said she was cuttin' a ham-bone in two an' hurt her han'. He showed the man a ring, an' asked him would he own it. He said he would. He said that was his wife ring he bought him [her(?)] befo' dey was married. So they went in de room an' asked her was dat her ring. She said it was not. Then they looked, an' her right han' was cut off at de wrist."[52]

For the sake of convenience we may here consider an extraordinary document in which a house is rendered uninhabitable by the machinations of a shape-shifting witch. In a volume of more than three hundred pages the author—one M. V. Ingram—records, partly in his own, partly in the words of others, a series of fearsome happenings which illustrate several points of the witchcraft superstition as it existed a century ago in North Carolina and

---

[52] *J. A. F.-L.*, xxx, 196. For another excellent version, from the Big Smoky Mountains, see *J. A. F.-L.*, vii (1894), 115. Here the mill is haunted with a single witch-cat, but in an account from Chestertown, Maryland, a mill is haunted by "a lot of black cats," one of which turns out to be the miller's wife when one of its front paws is cut off by the watcher (*J. A. F.-L.*, xii (1899), 68 f.). Scot (*op. cit.*, p. 72) tells of a man who, while in the form of a wolf, "had his wolves feet cut off, and in a moment ... became a man without hands or feet." For other parallels, see Harvard *Studies and Notes*, viii, 227, n. 2. Mills have long been favorite haunts of supernatural beings. Robin Goodfellow frequents mills (*Percy Soc.*, ix, 114).

eastern Tennessee. The title-page reads: AN AUTHENTICATED HISTORY OF THE FAMOUS *BELL WITCH. The Wonder of the 19th Century, and Unexplained Phenomenon of the Christian Era.* The Mysterious Talking Goblin that Terrorized the West End of Robertson County, Tennessee, Tormenting John Bell to His Death. THE STORY OF BETSY BELL, HER LOVER AND THE HAUNTING SPHINX. Copyrighted, 1894, By M. V. INGRAM, CLARKSVILLE, TENN. Clarksville, Tenn.: Wm. P. Titus, Agt., Printer and Binder.[53]

The book gives what purports to be an accurate account of the experiences of certain members of the family of John Bell, who in 1804 moved to Robertson County, Tennessee,[54] from Halifax County, North Carolina. The author affirms that he "only assumes to compile the data, formally presenting the history of this greatest of all mysteries, just as the matter is furnished to hand, written by Williams Bell, a member of the family, some fifty years ago, together with other corroborative testimony by men of irreproachable character and unquestionable veracity" (p. 6 f.). Appended to Mr. Ingram's compilation are detailed reports of interviews with his informants, several letters from persons able to speak with authority, and an extended history of "Our Family Trouble" by Richard Williams, son of the unfortunate John Bell.

Mr. Ingram declines to propound any theory regarding the cause of the phenomena he records, nor has he, he affirms, "any opinion to advance concerning witchcraft, sorcery, spiritualism or psychology in any form"; yet he devotes a chapter of thirty pages to the presentation of a mass of evidence tending to establish the reality of supernatural phenomena. He cites the Bible and John Wesley, Richard Watson, Adam Clarke, and other commentators, as well as several modern instances, of which the mysterious "rocking of Dr. William Smith's cradle, which occurred in 1840, in Lynchburg, Va.," may serve as an example.

[53] In the copy before me a slip of paper bearing the words SETLIFF & Co., NASHVILLE, TENN., is pasted over the name of the printer and that of the place of publication.

[54] According to the author, the Bell homestead was situated on the south bank of the Red River, about a mile from the spot now occupied by Adams Station, the latter being some forty miles north of Nashville, on the southeastern branch of the Louisville and Nashville (the old Edgefield and Kentucky) Rail Road (pp. 17, 37).

After a brief sketch of the social and religious life of the simple, frontier community in which the Bell family settled, Mr. Ingram describes a long series of persecutions which John Bell and his daughter Betsy suffered at the hands of an invisible being who took up its abode at the Bell homestead and made itself a general nuisance.[55] It first revealed its presence in 1817, and, when questioned regarding its origin, claimed to have come from North Carolina. Sometimes alone, sometimes accompanied by four other airy personages denominated Blackdog, Mathematics, Cypocryphy, and Jerusalem,[56] it filled the house with wild laughter, profane language, and coarse jests. The smacking of unseen lips and strange sounds "like rats gnawing the bed posts ... dogs fighting ... or trace chains dragging over the floor" made sleep impossible. Covers were pulled from the beds, chairs were overturned, "chunks of wood and stones" fell unexpectedly in the path of the farm laborers, ghostly lights flitted around the house, and various members of the family were struck by unseen hands. At times the demonic family sang sweetly, and the "witch" quoted Scripture with astonishing accuracy. In 1817 "Mr. Bell, while walking through his corn field, was confronted by a strange animal, unlike any he had ever seen, sitting in a corn row, gazing steadfastly at him as he approached nearer. He concluded that it was probably a dog, and having his gun in hand, shot at it, when the animal ran off. Some days after, in the late afternoon, Drew Bell observed a very large fowl, which he supposed to be a wild turkey, as it perched upon the fence, and ran in the house for a gun to kill it. As he approached within shooting distance, the bird flapped its wings and sailed away, and then he was mystified in discovering that it was not a turkey, but some unknown bird of extraordinary size. Betsy walked out one evening soon after this

---

[55] At intervals the "witch" frequented other places in the community, among them Fort's mill, about a mile from John Bell's house. The machinery was often heard running at night after the miller had left the building (p. 61).

[56] Anonymos, Dicke, Bonjour, Wilkin, Lustie Jollie-Jenkin, Corner-Cap, Pippin, and such like appear in a list of names of devils from Harsnet's *Declaration of Egregious Popish Impostures* (L., 1603), famous because of its association with Shakespeare's *King Lear* (cf. *N. & Q.*, Sec. Ser., VII [1859], 144). See further Ashton, *The Devil in Britain and America*, p. 160 ff.

with the children, among the big forest trees near the house, and saw something which she described as a pretty little girl dressed in green, swinging to a limb of a tall oak. Then came Dean, the [negro] servant, reporting that a large black dog came in the road in front of him at a certain place, every night that he visited his wife Kate, who belonged to Alex. Gunn [a neighbor], and trotted along before him to the cabin door and then disappeared" (p. 25).[57] "The Goblin's favorite form, however, was that of a rabbit, . . . the hare ghost took malicious pleasure in hopping out into the road, showing itself to every one who passed through [the lane in front of the house]."[58]

Witch-doctors and other persons attempted repeatedly to discover the cause of the strange events, but to no purpose. "The want of some satisfactory explanation or the failure of all investigators to throw light on the witch mystery, gave rise to the speculative idea that John and Drew Bell had learned ventriloquism and some subtle art. . . , and taught the same to their sister Betsy, for the purpose of attracting people and making money" (p. 41), but, as investigation showed, it was no such matter.

The unseen visitor's own account of itself was far from satisfactory. At one time it claimed to be the spirit of a child buried in North Carolina. At another it was a disturbed ghost seeking a lost tooth under the Bell house. When, however, the flooring was removed and the dirt sifted, no tooth was found, and a mocking voice from the air declared it was "all a joke to fool 'Old Jack'," as the "witch" called John Bell. On another occasion it was the ghost of an early settler, come back to reveal the whereabouts of hid treasure; but the money was not found, and the "witch"

[57] Later in the book the author gives an account of an interview with the negro's sister-in-law, in which the latter said that Dean carried a "witch-ball" to protect him from evil influences, and that the dog, when seen by him on another occasion, had two heads (p. 222).

[58] "This same rabbit," adds Mr. Ingram with a faint suggestion of humor, "is there plentifully to this day, and can't be exterminated. Very few men know a witch rabbit; only experts can distinguish it from the ordinary molly cotton tail. The experts in that section, however, are numerous, and no one to this good day will eat a rabbit that has a black spot on the bottom of its felt hind foot. When the spot is found, the foot is carefully cut off and placed in the hip pocket, and the body buried on the north side of an old log" (p. 57).

ridiculed the seekers. Again it called itself "old Kate Batts' witch," an appellation by which it was afterwards known.

Kate Batts was a sort of gigantic Mrs. Malaprop, whose propensity for using long words and whose evil tongue made her at once the laughing stock and the terror of the neighborhood. After the "witch's" assertion it was recalled not only that Mrs. Batts had an old grudge against John Bell, but also that certain events connected with her history savored strongly of witchcraft. She had a habit of " begging a brass pin of every woman she met, which trifle," adds the author, "was supposed to give her power over the donor" (p. 63). "The most incontrovertible evidence [however] was that a certain girl in the vicinity was given the task of churning, and after working the dasher diligently for two hours without reward, and no sign of butter coming, she declared that old Kate Batts had bewitched the milk and she determined to burn her. Carrying out this decision, she stuck an iron poker in the fire, and after it had come to a white heat, she soused the iron into the milk, setting the churn away; then making some excuse for the visit, she called on Aunt Kate to ascertain the result of her experiment, and found Mrs. Batts sitting in the corner nursing a burnt hand, which had been badly blistered through a mistake in taking the poker by the hot end that morning" (p. 69 f.). Mrs. Batts violently denied all connection with the Bell "witch," and the matter was never brought to a test.

Whatever may have been the cause of the phenomena described by Mr. Ingram, the persecution of the "witch" brought naught but sorrow to the Bells. The father became despondent and in 1820 died; Betsy was forced to give up her lover, and the household was finally broken up.

The following clipping, taken apparently from the query column of the Nashville, Tennessee, *Banner*, has some bearing on the events described in Mr. Ingram's book:

"'Is there such a thing as a Bell Witch near Springfield, Tenn.? If so, please tell some of its doings of the past.'

"A great many of the most reputable among the older citizens of Springfield and Robertson County are convinced that there was an unexplainable manifestation of some sort which was generally regarded as a ghost, and which came to be called the Bell Witch. It was said to jump on the steeds of men returning home from Springfield after dark, shriek in an unearthly manner and of other alarming things (sic). In the eighties, when there was a recurrence of what was supposed to be the Bell Witch manifestations, the *Banner* sent Mr. John C. Cooke to investigate. He concluded that there was not at that time any supernatural manifestation, though he heard noises that were not explained. Mr. Cook (sic) is still a member of the *Banner* staff. While he does not accept the ghost theory, he is convinced that there was a mysterious something that alarmed many of the most intelligent people of that community. Mr. Martin V. Ingram of Clarksville wrote a book undertaking to give all the facts and circumstances in which the Bell Witch figured, and this book can probably be obtained from second-hand book dealers."

The student of folk-lore will recognize at once that we are here [59] dealing with a series of phenomena long associated with haunted houses.[60] Buildings rendered uninhabitable by terrorizing agencies have existed in fact from time immemorial, and their horrors have formed the basis of skeptical or sympathetic treatment from the ancient classical drama to the more modern Gothic romance and the contemporary penny-dreadful. Moreover, it should be observed that, although houses may be haunted by vampires, ghosts, and other uncanny beings not necessarily associated with witchcraft, the ills which befall the occupants have frequently been attributed to *maleficium*. During the great period of witch mania in Western Europe many buildings in the British Isles and on the Continent were disturbed by the Devil or his human emissaries. A few well authenticated instances of English and American houses troubled by diabolic forces will make it obvious that the agency responsible for the misfortunes of the Bell family did but illustrate the excessive conservativeness with which the powers of evil stick to tradition.

[59] Events closely resembling those described in *The Bell Witch* are outlined by E. B. Miles in a series of sketches of life in the Cumberlands (*The Spirit of the Mountains*, p. 108 ff.). They concern "an old woman, or the spirit of one," who annoyed the family of Beaver. As a result of the visitations the head of the family pined and died.

[60] On demon- and witch-haunted houses, see Kittredge, Harvard *Studies and Notes*, VIII, 227, n. 2; Chas. Mackay, *Memoirs of Extraordinary Popular Delusions*, London, 1869, p. 217 ff.; J. H. Ingram, *The Haunted Homes and Family Traditions of Great Britain*, London, 1888; Andrew Lang, *Book of Dreams and Ghosts*, Longmans, 1897, p. 187 ff. Compare the ill-disposed haunting spirits in Wirt Sikes, *British Goblins*, London, 1880, p. 143 ff.; Catherine Crowe, *The Night Side of Nature*, ed., E. A. Baker, London and New York, 1904, p. 302 ff.

In 1649 the Parliamentary commissioners who had established themselves in the palace of Woodstock for the purpose of surveying the royal demesne after the execution of Charles I, were so pestered by strange noises, unaccountable movements of furniture, and other extraordinary phenomena, that they gave up the work.[61] About the middle of the century a family living at Stratford-Bow was annoyed by an invisible agency which disarranged the furniture and threw stones and bricks through the window. An eyewitness was convinced that "it was neither the tricks of Waggs, nor the fancy of a Woman, but the mad frolicks of Witches and Daemons. Which they of the house being fully persuaded of, roasted a Bed-staff, upon which an old Woman, a suspected Witch, came to the House, and was apprehended, but escaped the Law. But the House after was so ill haunted in all the Rooms, upper and lower, that the House stood empty for a long time."[62] In 1654-5 the family of Gilbert Campbell, a weaver living in Galloway, Scotland, underwent a series of similar annoyances as the result of Campbell's having refused alms to a sturdy beggar named Alexander Agnew, "who afterwards was hanged at *Dumfries*, for Blasphemy." When questioned by the minister, an invisible demon confessed that he was the author of the trouble and showed himself even more learned in the Scriptures than did Kate Batts.[63] About the year 1661 a series of persecutions strikingly similar to those described in *The Bell Witch* were suffered by the household of Mr. John Mompesson, of Tedworth, Wilts. An invisible force pulled the children's hair and night-clothes and even lifted the children themselves bodily out of bed, scattered the grandmother's garments and hid her bible in the hearth, moved furniture, opened and shut doors, and

---

[61] The commissioners blamed the disturbance on the Devil, but an eighteenth-century tradition, which it must be admitted is not above suspicion, has it that the perpetrator was one John Collins, a loyalist who, by concealing his real opinions secured a place with the commission and who was well acquainted with the trap-doors and secret passages of the building. Cf. Ashton, *op. cit.*, p. 45 f.; Mackay, *Memoirs*, p. 224. The story of the commissioners' experiences is told in a pamphlet entitled *The Just Devil of Woodstock*, etc., London, 1660 (whence it is repeated by Ashton, *op. cit.*, p. 28 ff.); in Glanvill's *Sadduc. Triumph.*, p. 403 ff. (whence it is summarized by Mackay, *Memoirs*, p. 221 ff.), and in Wright's *Narratives*, II, p. 167 ff.

[62] *Sadduc. Triumph.*, p. 361 ff.

[63] *Ibid.*, p. 412 ff.; Ashton, *The Devil in Britain and America*, p. 73 ff.

sprinkled ashes in the beds. Mysterious sounds, at times resembling the beat of a drum, resounded through the house, music was heard in the chimney, and once lights were seen. " One of them [the lights] came into Mr. Mompesson's Chamber, which seemed blue and glimmering, and caused great stiffness in the Eyes of those that saw it." On the morning after a particularly violent exhibition of preternaturalism tracks of claws were seen in the ashes, and sulphurous and otherwise noisome odors filled the house. The invisible disturber, when questioned as to its identity, indicated that it was Satan acting in the service of a drummer whom Mr. Mompesson had previously arrested for vagrancy. The drummer was accordingly tried for witchcraft and deported. Many persons visited the house out of pious curiosity, and skeptics whispered that the sorely vexed gentleman had got up the report " as a trick to get Money from those that came to see the Prodigy," but the accusation was denied by the orthodox. The doings of the " Daemon of Tedworth " were important enough to attract the attention of the famous Joseph Glanvill, who devoted to them a dissertation.[64] The story is retold in the " Choice Collection of Modern Relations " appended by Henry More to Glanvill's notable defence of witchcraft, *Sadducismus Triumphatus*,[65] whence it is summarized as valuable evidence of the existence of witches by Increase Mather in his *Remarkable Providences*, published at Boston in 1684.[66]

That in house-haunting as in other matters pertaining to their unhallowed profession, the witches of the New World followed the lead of their exemplars across the Atlantic, will be recalled at once by all readers of early New England literature, especially Increase Mather's book just referred to and his famous son Cotton's *Wonders of the Invisible World*. To multiply instances is unnecessary. The cases enumerated above demonstrate clearly that the Bell witch, far from exciting wonder by the novelty of her tactics, is remarkable only for her lack of invention.

[64] *Palpable Evidence of Spirits and Witchcraft*. The only copy the writer has seen was published in London in 1668. Glanvill's account is repeated by Ashton, op. cit., p. 47 ff.

[65] P. 270 ff. of the 1726 edition. For other seventeenth-century evidence, see Ashton, op. cit., p. 64 ff.; Sadduc. Triumph., p. 366 ff. See further Wright, *Narratives*, II, p. 336 ff.

[66] Cf. Burr, *Narratives*, p. 32 f.

Returning to the matter of witch transformation, we observe that witches are constantly confused with fairies [67] and other shape-shifters, and that consequently, like the beautiful and immortal *fées* of mediaeval romance, they sometimes assume the form of deer. The account given below was received from the Virginia negress who furnished the data on witch marks.[68] A woman who was a witch became enamored of a man on a neighboring plantation, and, in order to approach him, changed herself into a doe and appeared at his "hog-feedin'" place, whither she knew he came daily to bring corn to his stock. The man, supposing the animal to be an ordinary deer, shot at it, but without effect. He then loaded his gun with "a four-pence-ha'-penny cut into four parts," [69] and succeeded in shooting off one of the doe's feet. Imbedded in the hoof he found a ring which he recognized as belonging to his would-be mistress. He afterwards discovered that the woman was minus a hand.

The following story from Beaufort County, North Carolina, is condensed from a narrative communicated by Rev. G. Calvin Campbell (colored), who writes that the tradition has long been current in that district. An old woman who lived in a dilapidated log house near a swamp some distance from the public road, made a practice of turning herself into a deer, in which form she was frequently chased by a pack of hounds belonging to certain hunters in the community. The deer always followed the same trail and disappeared at the same place. Since the transformed witch invariably ran along a path used by real deer, the hunters were for a long time deceived. When, however, several of the best marksmen in the county had shot at the animal unsuccessfully, the hunters suspected that they really had to do with the old hag in disguise. They accordingly mixed silver with their buck-shot, and when next they shot at the witch-deer, they succeeded in wounding it. The animal escaped and was never seen again.

[67] For many examples, see Sir Walter Scott, *Letters on Demonology*, etc., edn. cit., p. 118 ff. See further Reginald Scot, op. cit., p. 19, where the witches' Sabbath is identified with the fairies' dance, and the "ladie of the fairies" is said to preside with the Devil at witch meetings. Glanvill's *Sadduc. Triumph.* (edn. cit., p. 356 ff.) contains a story which clearly illustrates how easily witches are confused with fairy beings.

[68] Cf. *J. A. F.-L.*, XXII (1909), 251 f.

[69] A small silver coin, said to be worth six and a quarter cents.

"They say that the suspected old woman had a sore limb for a long time after this and that it could not be cured."

In Scott County, Tennessee, a hunter whose gun had been bewitched, tried in vain to kill a mysterious deer which waited for him to shoot three times before running away. By the advice of a witch-doctor he used as a mark a tree to which he gave the name of the woman suspected of having spelled the weapon. When the tree was struck, the woman cried out and the charm was broken.[70] The animal here referred to is doubtless kin to the supernatural stag which roams the mountains in various parts of the Alleghanies and which has so often eluded the most skillful hunters.[71]

---

[70] *J. A. F.-L.*, XIII (1900), 209 f. For other methods of counteracting the charms placed by witches upon weapons, see Andrée, *Ethnographische Parallellen u. Vergleiche*, p. 42 ff. Eph Tucker (on whom, see above, p. 231), told Mr. Thomas Smith a story in which a witch appeared in the form of a bear, but I know of no other case in North Carolina. It seems that 'Ole Ferro' had taken a dislike to a certain man in the community. One night the man saw "a big thing like a bear a-walkin' the jist (joists) over his bed all night. The man said he tried to shoot the thing, but his gun wouldn't shoot, and he had to set there and watch that ole bear or whatever it wuz all night a-walkin' on the jist back'ards and for'ards right over his bed."

[71] For an account of this animal, see *J. A. F.-L.*, XIII (1900), 211. For the proper method of killing it, see *J. A. F.-L.*, III (1890), 202; and *infra*, pp. 284 f. Cf. Horace Kephart, *Our Southern Highlanders*, Outing Pub. Co., 1913, p. 91. See further *J. A. F.-L.*, VII (1894), 109, where reference is made to the black dog of the vale of Chatata, the gray wolf seen at midnight where the road from West Virginia crosses Piney Ridge, the headless bull of southeastern Tennessee, and the bleeding horse of the Smoky Mountains of Georgia. On these, see also Chas. H. Skinner, *Myths and Legends of Our Own Land*, Lippincott, II [N. D.], 68 f. Supernatural appearances of a similar character are reported in a recent communication to the North Carolina Folk-Lore Society by Mr. Thomas Smith, of Zionville. One of these is connected with the "Big Laurel," a dense jungle of "laurel," "ivy," and other mountain shrubs in the western part of Watauga County. The appearance of "hants" in this district is attested by many reliable citizens, among whom, says Mr. Smith, is Dr. Rivers, formerly a well known physician of Boone. While traversing the Laurel one morning just before daylight a few years after the Civil War, the doctor saw a strange man seated on a gray horse exactly like his own. A moment later horse and man had vanished. Not long afterwards the doctor died, and it was believed that the spectral horseman had come as a warning of his approaching demise. One of Mr. Smith's informants accounts for the large number of "hants" in the district by the suggestion

that "the Indians who used to camp here of a summer may have murdered one of their tribe and buried him in or near the Laurel." The scene of another of Mr. Smith's stories is a spring situated by the roadside a mile east of Watauga River. "The reputation of the place for being haunted is known to scores of people." One of them, Andrew Wilson, a reliable farmer living near Zionville, tells the following: "I was coming from Elk Park one night about twenty years ago. I'd been there with a load of lumber. When I come to the spring where the ghosts are seen, I stopped to let my horses drink. The horses wouldn't drink, and they seemed like they was skeered. Just then I looked ahead of me in the road and seed a man a-standing there. I could see he had shiny brass buttons on his coat like a soldier. Thinking it was somebody, I says, 'Howdy?' It didn't make no reply; so I spoke agin, but it didn't notice me. I watched it several minutes, and while I was a-gazin' at it, the thing jist seemed to fade away, and I could never see where it went to. I tell ye, I drove off from there in a hurry. But I didn't see the worst things that are seen there," continued Mr. Wilson. "Why, lots and lots of people have passed there of nights and seed the strangest things you ever heard tell of. They first see seven 'possums cross the road and go into a laurel thicket near the spring; then seven dogs follow right after the 'possums; then seven men cross the road right after the dogs into the laurel; and right after the men they see seven coffins sail across the road into the laurel thicket. I know of men who say they have seed all them skeery hants. Yes, there was men murdered there before the War; that's what causes them strange things to be seed." Several of Mr. Smith's stories concern a headless dog that used to emerge from a pile of rocks marking the site of an old school-house near the road from Cove Creek to Brushy Fork. Though the cause of the dog's appearing at just this place has never been discovered, it has been hinted that a traveler and his dog were killed there by robbers and buried under the school-house. Several reliable persons living on Cove Creek have heard of or seen the headless dog. On one occation the animal followed a man who was passing along the road on horseback after dark. The traveller put spurs to his horse, but the dog followed swiftly and leaped on the horse's back. The frightened rider, on looking over his shoulder, saw the creature sitting behind him, its bloody neck almost touching his back. By the time he had reached a settlement several miles distant, the dog had disappeared. Cf. Sikes, *British Goblins*, p. 168 ff. Some thirty years ago three young men were returning home one night from a "meetin'" on Brushy Fork. Some distance beyond the pile of rocks, one of the company, happening to glance behind, saw a large black dog following them. The animal was headless, and although the moon shone bright, it cast no shadow. The young men hurried on, but the dog overtook them, and even ran ahead, gamboling and rolling at their feet. One of them struck it with his cane, but the stick passed through its body as through thin air. When they reached a creek two miles farther on, the apparition turned back, though with evident reluctance. In ante-bellum days the negroes of certain parts of South Carolina knew a "hant" called "Plat-eye," which generally appeared in the form of a dog (*J. A. F.-L.,*

As Professor John M. McBryde pointed out some years ago,[72] the hare has long figured in the mythology of various peoples. Owing doubtless to its generally uncanny character, it served as a disguise for witches during the sixteenth and seventeenth centuries,[73] and today it is connected with several omens of good or ill fortune. For example, in the mountains of North Carolina, as elsewhere in the United States, it is bad luck for a rabbit to cross the path in front of a traveller.[74] "The left hind foot of a grave-

---

xxvii (1914), 248). For similar superstitions on the "Eastern Shore" of Virginia, see J. C. Wise, Ye Kingdome of Accawmacke, p. 334. Mr. Coon records a belief, current formerly in Lincoln County, North Carolina, that witches sometimes walked the rail fences on all fours, "displaying large, flaming red eyes." In 1612 a witness in an English witchcraft trial deposed that a witch had appeared to her in the form of a black dog with two legs and had tried to persuade her to drown herself (Thomas Wright, Narratives, ii, 128). For additional seventeenth century evidence, see Glanvil, op. cit., 295; A. M. Gummere, Witchcraft and Quakerism, Phila. and London, 1908, p. 31. The story about Dr. Rivers suggests the whole class of supernatural warnings of approaching death, of which many examples are said to be current in North Carolina. One of these, recorded by Mr. Smith, concerns 'Little Booney' Potter, a desperate character who formerly lived in North Fork township and who was killed in an encounter with a sheriff's posse. A few nights before Potter's death the desperado's bed-fellow was terrified by "somthin' big and heavy [that] came and sot down right on the bed." Although the thing did not leave until nearly daylight, Potter slept undisturbed. Later his companion said he was sure the visitation had foretold Potter's death. It would be interesting to discover whether phantom ships are still seen along the Carolina coast. Lawson (writing early in the eighteenth century) records a report "the truth of [which] has been affirmed to me, by men of the best Credit in the Country," "that the Ship which brought the first Colonies, does often appear amongst them [the people of Roanoke Island] under sail, in a most gallant Posture, which they call Sir Walter Raleigh's Ship" (op. cit., p. 34). A shadowy craft used to appear on the Rappahannock River, Va. (Skinner, Myths and Legends of Our Own Land, ii, 71).

[72] Sewanee Rev., April, 1911. Cf. "Mythology of All Races," x (North American), p. 67.

[73] In 1663 a witch named Julian Cox, of Somersetshire, England, was accused of transforming herself into a hare (Glanvil, op. cit., p. 326). In another account a ghost assumes the form of a hare (Ibid., p. 337 f.) See further Notestein, op. cit., p. 171; Matthew Hopkins, Discovery of Witches, London, 1647, p. 2. The devil's mark is sometimes said to resemble the impression of a hare's foot (Black, Folk-Medicine, p. 155).

[74] J. A. F.-L., xx (1907), 245. Cf. So. Workman, xxxiii (1904), 52; xxxv, 634. In County Clare, Ireland, both fairies and witches take the

yard rabbit killed in the dark of the moon" brings good fortune,[75] and, as every reader of Uncle Remus knows, a graveyard rabbit, like a witch, cannot be killed with ordinary shot.

The bad reputation of toads is of extremely long standing,[76] and their association with suspected witches as familiars was constantly introduced as evidence before courts of justice during the sixteenth and seventeenth centuries.[77] We all remember that one of the ingredients of the witches' caldron in *Macbeth* was a

> Toad, that under cold stone
> Days and nights has thirty-one
> Sweltered venom sleeping got,

and that when Milton's Satan wished to tempt Eve, he "squat like a toad" at her ear. Today American witches who take the form of toads seem to be rare,[78] but it is well known in western North Carolina that, if you kill a toad, your cows will give bloody

---

form of rabbits (*Folk-Lore*, XXI (1910), 483; XXII, 449). An Irish story tells how a hare bitten by hounds ran into a cottage, "where an old woman was found torn behind" (*Folk-Lore*, XXIII (1912), 214).

[75] *J. A. F.-L.*, XXVII (1914), 247 (S. C.-negro?). On the rabbit in popular lore, see Black, *op. cit.*, p. 154 f; Karl Knortz, *Zur amerikanischen Volkskunde*, Tübingen, 1905, p. 10; *Amerikanischer Aberglaube der Gegenwart*, Leipzig, 1913, p. 35 ff.

[76] On the frog and the toad in literature and folk-lore, see Karl Knortz, *Reptilien u. Amphibien in Sage, Sitte u. Literatur*, Annaberg (Sachsen), 1911, pp. 30 ff., 69 ff.

[77] Cf. Notestein, *op. cit.*, pp. 160 ff., 184, 261. There seem to be few American witches who take the form of snakes. A Guilford County story tells of a little girl who had a snake with which she used to eat. The lives of the two were so intimately connected that, when the snake was killed, the girl died (*J. A. F.-L.*, XXX, 185). On a snake woman married to a Maryland man, see *J. A. F.-L.*, XII (1899), 68 f. Cf. the same journal, vol. XII, 228 ff.; *So. Workman*, XXIX (1900), 180. Lawson reports that the Indians of North Carolina avoided killing a snake for fear "some of the Serpents Kindred would kill some of the Savages Relations that should destroy him" (*op. cit.*, p. 124). He also records an Indian tradition regarding a demon snake that devoured "Great Canoes full of Indians, at a time" (*op. cit.*, p. 127). Cf. Kittredge, *The Old Farmer*, p. 108. Heads, skins, and oil of snakes are, of course, common in the practice of witchcraft and of popular medicine in the South. See *infra*, p. 265 ff.

[78] For an instance, see *J. A. F.-L.*, XVII (1904), 265. A Guilford County story tells of a woman who had a diabolical stuffed frog (*J. A. F.-L.*, XXX, 183 f.-negro).

milk,[79]—a misfortune which often results from the machinations of witches. According to a peculiar belief current not long ago in the Alleghany Mountains, "toads are often kept by witches instead of chickens, and their eggs are known from the fact that it is very difficult to break their shells. When these creatures are dilatory in laying, the witch switches them, and then for a time the toads become very prolific. Most frequently she keeps the reptiles in a hollow stump."[80] Because of their supposed venomous character toads were formerly much used in the practice of medicine to drive out less virulent poisons, and it is still a popular belief in eastern North Carolina that a live toad-frog cut in two and applied to the bite of a mad dog will draw out the venom.[81]

Throughout the Southern States the "screech-owl," like the raven of European tradition, is regarded with suspicion.[82] It is used as a disguise by witches, and the charms to prevent its "hollo'ing" are also effective against witchcraft.[83]

[79] *J. A. F.-L.*, xx (1907), 244. If you kill frogs, your cows will go dry (*J. A. F.-L.*, vii (1894), 306 (Ga.). In Knott County, Ky., as in eastern Virginia and elsewhere in the United States, handling toads causes warts on the hand. The excrescences may be removed by selling them to a witch, who will pay for them with pins (*J. A. F.-L.*, xxiv, 319). For other ways of removing warts, see *infra*, pp. 261 f. In New England handling toads causes freckles (F. D. Bergen, *Animal and Plant Lore*, p. 88). Cf. *Pop. Sci. Mo.*, xxxix (1891), 378. For a toad to enter the house is a sure sign of approaching death (*So. Workman*, xxxiii [1904], 51; Ala.-negro). Among the mountain whites of the South witches may be prevented from entering a house by drawing a picture of a frog's foot on the entrance (*J. A. F.-L.*, vii (1894), 113). Cf. the same journal, vol. iv (1891), 324. On the magical properties of the toad, see F. D. Bergen, *op. cit.*, p. 126.

[80] *J. A. F.-L.*, vii (1894), 116.

[81] In 1657 Sir Kenelm Digby wrote: "The Farcy is a venemous and contagious humor within the body of a Horse: hang a toad about the neck of the Horse in a little bag and he will be cured infallibly: the Toad, which is the stronger poyson, drawing to it the venome which was within the Horse." *Of the Sympathetick Powder, A Discourse in Solemn Assembly, at Montpellier. Made in French, by Sir Kenelm Digby, Knight, 1657,* London, 1669, p. 176. Cf. *N. Y. Med. J.*, Feby. 19, 1916. See further, *infra*, p. 253, n. 97.

[82] See *J. A. F.-L.*, vii (1894), 305; xii (1899), 269 (Ga.). Cf. vol. vi (1893), 70 (N. H.).

[83] Cf. F. D. Bergen, *Animal and Plant Lore*, p. 20. Brickell asserts that in his day the screech-owl was eaten by Indians and negroes, that its flesh cures palsy and melancholy, and that its grease strengthens the eyesight (*Natural History*, edn. cit., p. 178 f.).

In order to change from human into animal form, witches usually rub themselves with an ointment—a method which, it will be recalled, was used by Phoebe Ward, the Northampton County witch. Early recipes often call for grease distilled from corpses as one of the chief ingredients of witch ointment;[84] today among the negroes of Georgia "witch-butter" may be prepared from the fat of graveyard snakes (descendants of the original serpent in the Garden of Eden).[85]

From time immemorial witches have been endowed with varied and extensive powers of venting their malignancy upon humanity. "If it were true that witches confesse, or that all writers write, or that witchmongers report, or that fooles beleeve," wrote Reginald Scot, "we should never have butter in the chearne, nor cow in the close, nor corne in the field, nor faire weather abroad, nor health within doores."[86] Though the gradual spread of skepticism

---

[84] An early authority declares that the devil teaches witches "to make ointments of the bowels and members of children, whereby they ride in the aire, and accomplish all their desires" (Cf. Scot, *op. cit.*, 31). See further *infra*, p. 271, n. 162. In 1664 an English witch confessed that she and other witches were able to fly through the air by rubbing their foreheads and wrists with a 'raw smelling' oil furnished by a familiar spirit. (*Sadduc. Triumph.*, 297).

[85] Whoever rubs himself with the 'butter' becomes invisible, "'case Satan is 'bleged to stan' by folks what are greased wid his grease" (*J. A. F.-L.*, XXV (1912), 134). In 1828 Dr. Elisha Mitchell, while on a geological tour in the extreme northwestern portion of North Carolina, wrote to his wife: "While breakfast was getting ready heard an amusing account of an old man who determined the locality of ores by the mineral rod, and by his own account is very busy in digging for gold and silver taken from the Whites by the Indians, and laid up in 'subteranium chambers.' Said he greased his boots with dead men's tallow, and is prevented from getting the treasure out not by the little spirit with head no bigger than his two thumbs who came to blow the candle out, but by the big two horned devil himself." (*James Sprunt Historical Monograph*, No. 6 (1905), pub. by the University of North Carolina, p. 25). An amusing parallel to Lucius' misfortune in Apuleius' witch story was current not long ago in the Alleghany mountains. A witch's husband accidentally ate some corn-meal dough upon which his wife had put a spell in order to make her hens lay. As a result the poor fellow lost the power of speech and could only cackle like a hen (*J. A. F.-L.*, VII (1894), 116). Scot (*op. cit.*, p. 75 f.) quotes a story of a man who was transformed into an ass by eating bewitched eggs. On the general subject of transformation by means of witch-ointment, see Grimm, *Deut. Mythol.*, II, 895, n. 2.

[86] Cf. Addison's remarks in *The Spectator*, No. cxvii.

regarding the reality of black magic has within the last few generations somewhat circumscribed the witch's power of doing harm, many well authenticated cases of sickness and death of man and beast, still testify to the amazing vitality of the superstition.[87]

[87] For evidence, see O. M. Hueffer, *The Book of Witches*, London, 1908, Chaps. I and XVI; Linton, *op. cit.*, p. 426 ff.; *J. A. F.-L.*, II (1889), 233; III, 281 f.; X, 242 f.; XIV, 173 ff.; XXVII, 320 f. For a noteworthy early instance of wholesale death of human beings and cattle by witchcraft, see *The Northamptonshire Witches, Being a true and faithful Account of the Births, Educations, Lives, and Conversations of Elinor Shaw and Mary Phillips*, London, 1705, p. 6. The defendants were shown to have killed fifteen children, eight men, and six women, besides sundry cattle. See further Scot, *op. cit., passim;* the "Choice Collection of Modern Relations" appended to the fourth (1726) edition of Joseph Glanvill's *Sadducismus Triumphatus;* Grimm, *Deut. Mythol.*, II, 896 f. Cases of witchcraft are still brought from time to time before our courts of justice. See, for example, *J. A. F.-L.*, IV (1891), 325 (Pa.); VII, 144; XII, 289 f.; XVII, 90; XIX, 174 f.; cf. I, 30, note. Modern spiritualists, hypnotists, faith-healers, and fortune-tellers, as well as operators of many "confidence-games" have inherited much from the witches and wizards of the past. See "The Revival of Witchcraft," *Pop. Sci. Mon.*, XLIII (1893); Karl Knortz, *Zur amerikanischen Volkskunde*, p. 21 ff. Ever since the witch of Endor called up Samuel at the request of Saul, witches have sought to foretell the future by communing with the spirits of the dead. One instance is recorded of a North Carolina woman who asked the services of a male witch to raise the spirit of her dead husband so that she might learn where he had concealed his money (*J. A. F.-L.*, II (1889), 101). The story of Saul and the witch of Endor gave mediæval commentators a world of trouble. Cf. Scot, *op. cit.*, p. 111 ff., for many references. Are witches in North Carolina ever accused of raising storms? The charge was frequently made against witches three hundred years ago. See Scot, *op. cit.*, p. 47 f.; *Sadduc. Triumph.*, p. 397. Cf. Thomas Ady, *A Candle in the Dark*, London, 1656, p. 117 f. The early colonists of North Carolina believed that Indian conjurers could create storms of wind (Brickell, *op. cit.*, p. 370). An instance of a favorable wind created by a friendly Indian for the benefit of European sailors, is given in the *Colonial Records of North Carolina*, I (1886), 983. Cf. Colonel William Byrd's jocose reference in a letter of Oct. 22, 1735 (*Va. Mag. of Hist. and Biog.*, IX, 231). In New England Indian sorcerers, like the witch in *Macbeth* (I, iii, 10), could sink ships by gnawing holes in the bottom (*Old South Leaflets*, III, No. 54, p. 3). The power of influencing the weather has been attributed to the magicians of many peoples. A whole chapter has been devoted to the subject of weather-makers by Lieutenant F. S. Bassett in his *Sea Phantoms*, Chicago, 1892, p. 101 ff. Cf. Cockayne, *Leechdoms*, I, p. xlvii ff.; Martino Delrio, *Disquisitionum magicarum libri sex*, Moguntiae, 1617, Bk. II, xi, p. 140; Ashton, *op. cit.*, p. 80 ff.

Among the mountain whites of the South witches still injure the minds and bodies of men and women, stunt the growth of children, make cows give bloody milk, prevent the formation of butter and soap, and render fire-arms useless.[88] In a negro story from Guilford County a witch prevented a man's wife from having a child until the "trick," which was hidden in the chimney-corner, was found and the spell broken.[89] Mr. Coon, referring to conditions in Lincoln County during the first half of the last century, writes:

"Witches were frequently supposed not only to exert their evil influences upon human beings but also upon hogs, cattle, fowls, cats, dogs, and the like. If a cow went 'dry,' the witches were often charged with it. If the hogs or the cattle became diseased, the witches were supposed to have been exercising their spells and a witch doctor was called in to try to restore them to health again.... Sometimes a 'witch-man' would come to a shooting match and spoil the 'luck.' On such occasions the participants would immediately disperse, saying that no prizes could be won while a 'witch-man' was in their midst."

Mr. J. P. Arthur records a story told by the late Colonel Allen T. Davidson about a famous hunter named Neddy McFalls, who "traveled from Cataloochee to Waynesville to have a witch-doctor —a woman—remove a 'spell' he thought someone had put on his Gillespie rifle."[90]

The means by which Southern witches of today attain their ends are many. They vary all the way from incantations and other practices universally associated with witchcraft and obviously based originally on well recognized principles of magic, to cheap

---

[88] Cf. J. A. F.-L., VII (1894), 114; F. D. Berger, *Animal and Plant Lore*, p. 15 (Mitchell Co., N. C.). Among the Hudson Bay Indians, if a woman steps over a gun, the weapon becomes useless (Andrée, *op. cit.*, p. 43). In the North Carolina version of the familiar children's game beginning "Chick-ur-mur, chick-ur-mur, Cravy (or Crany, or Cramy) Crow" and known as "Hawk and Chickens" or "Hen and Chickens," an "Old Witch" take the place of the "Hawk" in attempting to steal the children (J. A. F.-L., V (1892), 119). For the English versions, see A. B. Gomme, *The Traditional Games of England, Scotland, and Ireland*, London, 1894, I, 201. Cf. vol. II, 391 ff., and W. W. Newell, *Games and Songs of American Children*, p. 215 ff.

[89] J. A. F.-L., XXX, 180.

[90] *Western North Carolina*, Raleigh, 1914, pp. 290, n. 10, 336. A fair estimate of the general value of Mr. Arthur's book is given by Archibald Henderson, Am. Hist. Rev., XX, 890.

"conjer" or "tricks," the rationale of which is difficult to determine. In some parts of the Alleghany Mountains there dwells a being who inveigles wayfarers into the power of demons and witches,[91] but ordinarily no such intermediary is necessary to bring the unfortunate mortal within the sphere of diabolical influence. The power of the "evil eye," so long an article of folk belief, is still known in the Alleghany Mountains,[92] but its exercise is said to be uncommon in the annals of English witchcraft.[93] Generally speaking, the practice of the black art is founded upon two well accepted principles of primitive society. The first, known as Sympathetic Magic, asserts that "any effect may be produced by imitating it"—a dictum based ultimately on the assumption that association in thought involves connection in reality.[94] According to the second, nails, hair, clothing and other articles of dress, and even the name are parts of the personality,[95] and, since to the primitive mind things once joined remain joined ever afterwards,[96] any intimate personal possession, in case it fall into the hands of an enemy, may be used by him to the detriment of the owner.[97]

[91] *J. A. F.-L.*, VII (1894), 110.
[92] *J. A. F.-L.*, VII (1894), 114; XIV, 42.
[93] Notestein, *op. cit.*, 111.
[94] Hartland, *Legend of Perseus*, London, II (1895), 64 ff.; Lang, *Myth, Ritual, and Religion*, I (1899), 96; F. T. Elworthy, *The Evil Eye*, London, 1895, 48. Cf. Kittredge, *The Old Farmer*, 115 f. Similarities of a purely accidental character are apparently responsible for a number of proverbs current among the Cumberland mountaineers. Hasty tempers and pepper are alike in that both are hot. Hence, "if you ain't bad-tempered you can't git pepper to bear." "If you're hairy about the arms and chest, you'll have good luck with hogs." According to Pliny, basil should be sowed with curses and ugly words (cf. Cockayne, *Leechdoms*, I, p. xv); the Southern highlander says, "If you don't cuss you'll never raise gourds" (E. B. Miles, *The Spirit of the Mountains*, p. 99). The principle underlying such sayings is exemplified in old-fashioned medicine under the name of the "Doctrine of Signatures." See T. J. Pettigrew, *On Superstitions Connected with the History and Practise of Medicine and Surgery*, Philadelphia, 1844, p. 33 f. Cf. *Vergleichende Volksmedizin*, ed., Hovorka and Kronfeld, II (1909), 858 f.
[95] For references, see *Modern Philology*, XII (1915), 622 f. Is it believed anywhere in North Carolina that the floating loaf of bread used to discover the whereabouts of a drowned body, should have the dead person's name written on it?
[96] Cf. Frazer, *Golden Bough*, I, 49 ff.
[97] On the other hand, if properly treated, it may cause great good to the

Faith in these two doctrines is responsible not only for the vast majority of witch practice, ancient and modern, but also for the efficacy of many counter-charms employed by "witch-doctors" and others who fight against magic with magic.[98]

These facts explain the universal fear of giving anything to a witch.[99] Whatever is done to the gift affects the giver. It is, however, scarcely less perilous to incur a witch's displeasure by refusing her request, for she has many strings to her diabolical fiddle, and she may find other ways of harming you.

The use of personal property for the purpose of injuring the owner should be well known in North Carolina. A few typical cases from neighboring territory are here given as illustrations of the general method of procedure. The following episode, said to have occurred in December, 1907, is given essentially as it appeared in the Richmond *Times-Dispatch,* because it illustrates so well, even in a reporter's "write-up," the psychology underlying the practice of witchcraft by sympathetic magic.

"A night or two ago ... a negro girl ran breathlessly up to an officer, and said she had been 'conjured.' 'Some gal's got the combin's of my hyar, an' nailed 'em to a tree,' she wept. 'I dunno how she got 'em, but she got 'em, and she's done nail 'em to a tree. ... Yo' white folks don' know 'bout sech things, ... but we cullud folks knows all erbout 'em. Dat gal sho' is got my combin's, cos' I'se got de headache. When yo' nails a gal's combin's to a tree, wid the combin's twisted roun' de nail, it sho'

---

original possessor. This doctrine explains the supposed efficacy of Sir Kenelm Digby's famous Sympathetic Powder, the use of which was expounded by the inventor in 1657. Sir Kenelm proved to his own satisfaction, as well as to that of many other persons, that a wound may be cured by treating with the powder the weapon which caused it or some object which had been in contact with the patient. For the modern explanation of the surprisingly large number of recoveries after the application of this method, see W. R. Riddell, *N. Y. Med. Journ.,* Feby. 19, 1916. Cf. Kittredge, *The Old Farmer,* 115 ff.; Karl Knortz, *Zur amerikanischen Volkskunde,* p. 24; Pettigrew, *Superstitions,* etc., p. 201 ff.

[98] On North Carolina witch-doctors of the early nineteenth century, see Brantley York, *Autobiog.,* 8. On the doctrine of sympathy in folk medicine, see Black, op. cit., 51 ff.; Dr. W. J. Hoffman, *Proc. Am. Phil. Soc.,* XXVI (1889), 330.

[99] *J. A. F.-L.,* IX (1896), 227. See also *Century Magazine,* XXXI (1885-6), 820; *J. A. F.-L.,* I (1888), 134 (Pa.); III, 206 (La.), 286 f.; IV, 254 (N. H.); XIV, 43 (Western Md.); Scot, op. cit., 5; *Sadduc. Triumph.,* 328; Ashton, *The Devil in Britain and America,* p. 64 ff.

gwine give yo' a headache, an' I'se got one arful bad. It's been achin' eber since dat gal got my combin's.' "[100]

A woman in Chestertown, Maryland, was terrified because someone had torn a piece out of her dress and "buried it against her."[101] In Georgia negroes "conjer" by getting the excrement of the person to be affected, boring a hole in a tree, putting the excrement into the hole, and driving in a plug. As a result the victim cannot defecate unless the peg is taken out and the tree cut down and burned on the spot.[102]

The same principle explains the terror with which the negroes and poor whites in some sections of the South regard the action of 'picking up tracks.' Because of their accessibility and their close association with the person, especially in country districts where there is much travelling on foot and many people go barefooted, foot-prints are especially liable to be used by witches in working their will upon the maker.[103] Some twenty years ago the

[100] Cf. *J. A. F.-L.*, XXII (1909), 253. If a bird gets your combings and makes a nest of them, you will have the headache. Cf. *So. Workman*, XL, 581 f.; *Ill. Med. Journ.*, Apr., 1917, 269 f. To make a cat remain in a new habitation, cut off and keep the last joint of her tail (*J. A. F.-L.*, XXVII (1914), 247) (S. C.). The following comes from eastern North Carolina: to prevent a ferocious dog from biting you, get a hair from the tail of the animal and bury it under your door-step. Never throw away your nail-clippings. Cf. Nassau, *Fetichism in West Africa*, p. 104.

[101] *J. A. F.-L.*, III (1890), 285 f. In one of the Lincoln (England) trials in 1618-19 it transpired that the witch had accomplished her diabolical purpose by dipping the victim's gloves in hot water, and then rubbing them on a cat and pricking them often (Thomas Wright, *Narratives*, II, 124; cf. Notestein, *op. cit.*, 134).

[102] *J. A. F.-L.*, XIV (1901), 179.

[103] For a highly illuminating discussion, see E. S. Hartland, *The Legend of Perseus*, II, 78 ff. It may be added that under certain circumstances tracks have a peculiar quality of permanence. The tracks of a horse which threw its rider while the latter was racing on Sunday, are said to be still visible on a road near Bath, N. C. In spite of many efforts to destroy them, they remain a permanent warning against the breach of the Second Commandment. Rev. G. Calvin Campbell (colored) writes that at a spot in Long Acre township, Beaufort County, North Carolina, there may still be seen the hoof-prints of a horse which threw its rider—an unregenerate man—during a race many years ago. According to current opinion, the ghost of the dead man comes every night and clears the tracks of whatever falls into them during the day. Although Bath is situated in Bath, not in Long Acre, township, both accounts doubtless refer to the same place.

practice was known in Georgia, and a writer in the *Journal of American Folk-Lore* for 1896 (p. 227 f.) tells how a country district in Mississippi was set by the ears because a negro woman had picked up the tracks of a man and his wife, carried them off, and buried them, interring dog's hair with the tracks of the man, cat's hair with those of the woman. "Hence the couple could no more live together than a dog and a cat." The writer is indebted to Mr. Wm. G. Caffey, formerly of Lowndes County, Alabama, for an account of how a negro on an Alabama plantation, who had picked up the tracks of another, was chased by a mob and was saved from rough handling only by the timely interference of the owner of the estate.[104] Mr. Stephenson writes that in Northampton County, North Carolina, conjure-bags sometimes contain, along with locks of hair and rocks, dirt from the tracks of the person to be injured. It is said that in Knott County, Kentucky, a lover may win his lady's favor by counting her steps up to the ninth, then taking some earth from the track made by her left shoe-heel, and carrying it in his pocket for nine days.[105] Here belongs also the superstition that a thief may be caught by driving a nail into one of his tracks. The effect is the same as if the nail were stuck into his foot. A string must therefore be tied around the head of the nail so that it may be drawn out when the offender is captured; otherwise he will die.[106]

In the absence of any article of personal property, the witch may establish direct connection with her victim by the use of a conventionalized image made of wood, dough, wax, or other available substance and representing the person to be affected—a device

---

[104] *J. A. F.-L.*, XXII (1909), 253. Cf. vol. IX (1896), 227.

[105] *J. A. F.-L.*, XXIV (1911), 321. The following extract from the collectanea of the North Carolina Folk-Lore Society is recommended to ladies who would know something of their future husbands: 'Starting on your right foot, take nine steps backwards. Take a handful of dirt from under the heel of your foot on the ninth step. In this dirt you will find a hair of the same color as that of the man you will marry.'

[106] *J. A. F.-L.*, VII (1894), 113. Similarly, if a sharp implement such as a knife, a fork, or a pin is stuck in the under side of the seat of a wooden-bottom chair or in the floor beneath it, any witch who sits on the chair will be impaled (cf. *J. A. F.-L.*, XI (1898), 76). The efficacy of this test was illustrated in the evidence against Florence Newton, accused of witchcraft at the Cork (Ireland) assizes in 1661 (*Sadduc. Triumph.*, p. 320).

familiar to all readers of Thomas Hardy's *Return of the Native* and Rossetti's ballad of "Sister Helen." The savage draws near to the god of his idolatry by driving a nail in his fetich.[107] The witch tortures her enemy by heating a little figure of wax or clay. This device was used by the witches of antiquity;[108] it was familiar to the early Germanic tribes;[109] it is often mentioned in the witchcraft trials of the sixteenth and seventeenth centuries;[110] and it is common among the African natives of the present day.[111] Among the evidences of witchcraft enumerated in Dalton's *Countrey Justice* is the following: "They [witches] have often pictures of clay or wax (like a man, &c. made of such as they would bewitch) found in their house, or which they roast, or bury in the earth, that as the picture consumes, so may the parties bewitched consume". (p. 277). According to a belief current as recently as 1896 in the remoter districts of Georgia, a witch may torture her enemy by baking an image of dough fashioned to represent the victim, and then sticking pins in it;[112] and a few years ago witches in southeastern Virginia were said to be guilty of much the same offence.

The principle of imitative action as applied to the practice of black magic is illustrated in an account of a witch-doctor who flourished in Johnston County, North Carolina, some three or four decades ago. Of this celebrity Professor William E. Dodd, of the University of Chicago, writes as follows:

"When I was a boy my father lived a little east of Clayton, North Carolina. There was a certain Doctor Duncan who lived somewhat more than two miles further east. He was known as a 'conjure doctor.' He was supposed to work marvellous cures upon people who had strange ail-

---

[107] Cf. E. S. Hartland, *Folklore; What is It and What is the Good of It* (Pop. Studies in Romance and Folk-Lore, 2), London, 1899, p. 17 f.; G. L. Gomme, *Handbook of Folklore*, London, 1890, p. 40 f.; Andrée, *op. cit.*, p. 8 ff.; Nassau, *Fetichism in West Africa*, p. 87 ff.

[108] Cf. F. T. Elworthy, *op. cit.*, 49, n.; Tacitus, *Annales*, II, 69.

[109] Cf. *J. A. F.-L.*, XXII (1909), 119 f.

[110] Cf. Notestein, *op. cit.*, pp. 109, n. 25, 215, 342, 378; St. John D. Seymour, *Irish Witchcraft and Demonology*, 1913, pp 147, 182; *Sadduc. Triumph.*, pp. 296, 391 f.

[111] Lang, *Myth, Ritual, and Religion*, I, 99. Cf. Jerome Dowd, *The Negro Races*, New York, 1907, p. 261; Mary H. Kingsley, *West African Studies*, I, 1899, p. 163.

[112] *J. A. F.-L.*, IX (1896), 227. Cf. *Century Mag.*, XXX (1885-6), 820.

ments. If men had been bewitched, he could remove the charm. If women wished their enemies to suffer, he could perform certain curious tricks and the victims would invariably begin their downward course. Negroes were especially subject to his cures and bewitchments. It was told me more than once that live frogs had been taken from negroes' swollen feet or legs by this wonder-worker. A certain negro woman was once caused to begin to stoop by this doctor. She continued to stoop till she finally got her feet and her head together, and died in that attitude. The doctor had only said a few words, heated a needle over a candle and put the point through its eye in the presence of the woman's enemy. Many and even more fanciful stories were told me of the marvellous man ' over the creek.' It would have been a joke to our household had it not been for the number of people from far and near, from distant states, who halted at our door, by day and by night, to ask the way to Dr. Duncan's."

The principle of sympathetic magic may also be applied in retaliation, since here, as in popular medicine, the rule *similia similibus curantur* holds good.[113] In Georgia a bewitched person may guard himself against further attacks for a year by making a dough effigy of the witch, tying a string around its neck, allowing the dough to rise, and then baking it. The witch is thus strangled.[114] From Mitchell County, North Carolina, comes the information that a vindictive person may wound his enemy by drawing his picture on a board and then shooting it.[115] Equally in accord with the most approved methods is the Pennsylvania prescription which substitutes for the drawing a hair from the witch's head wrapped in a piece of paper.[116]

[113] Compare the "Doctrine of Signatures," on which see above, p. 253, n. 94. Among the remnants of the Machapunga Indians in Dare and Hyde counties and on Roanoke Island, the bite of a rattlesnake may be cured by eating a piece of the snake. *Am. Anthrop.*, XVIII (1916), 273.

[114] *J. A. F.-L.*, IX (1896), 227. Cf. vol. XXV (1912), 134.

[115] F. D. Bergen, *Animal and Plant Lore*, p. 15. Mrs. Bergen states that the same method is used in Alabama. See further *J. A. F.-L.*, XIV (1901), 42. The fear of being photographed, encountered among savages and occasionally among civilized peoples, is based ultimately on the notion that the picture renders the person represented more liable to injury. Cf. Andrée, *op. cit.*, p. 18 ff.; R. E. Dennett, *At the Back of the Black Man's Mind*, London, 1906, p. 51.

[116] *J. A. F.-L.*, II (1889), 32. That such sympathetic remedies as those mentioned above are thoroughly in accord with the laws of nature and permissible under those of God, was maintained by Rev. Deodat Lawson in *Christ's Fidelity the Only Shield against Satan's Malignity*, a sermon delivered at Salem, Mass., in March, 1692. The second edition, consulted by the writer, appeared in 1704.

In the same category belong most cures for bewitched cattle. Among the mountain whites of the South, whatever is done to the animal affects the witch.[117] In general the contagion of witchcraft is checked if the first thing attacked is burned. Mr. James Mooney, in his article on "Folk-Lore in the Carolina Mountains," records the following instance, related by a lady as having occurred near Asheville within her own or her mother's recollection. "A valuable steer suddenly became sick without apparent cause, and the fact was attributed to witchcraft. The owner and his neighbors collected a pile of logs, laid the sick animal upon it while still alive, and burned it to ashes."[118] Mr. Joseph A. Haskell tells of another case which came under his observation while he was engaged in cotton-planting in North Carolina. One hot day he noticed the children of his negro overseer engaged in building a fire of leaves and sticks under the supervision of their father. The old darkey, on being asked the reason for the strange proceeding, replied, "The distemper has got my chickens and they are dying fast. Now when that happens, if you take a well one and burn it alive in the fork of the path it will cure the rest and no more will die." On another occasion the old negro even attempted to induce Mr. Haskell to burn a well mule "at the forks of the road" in order to stop the ravages of an epidemic among the stock on the plantation.[119] The following story from the mountains of Tennessee furnishes conclusive proof of the value of the method illustrated above. A man borrowed a boiler from a witch and refused to return it. In retaliation the hag "came every night and danced on him and also made one of his sheep die every day. He returned the boiler, but his ill luck continued." By the advice of a witch-doctor he took out the heart and lungs of the next sheep that died, performing the operation alone and in silence. He then carried the parts home and laid them on a bed of live coals. "The witch (who lived some distance away), immediately began to shriek, and some neighbors coming in and forcibly investigating, found her breast completely charred."[120] At the trial of Julian Cox, of Somersetshire, England, in 1663, a witness

---

[117] J. A. F.-L., VII (1894), 116.
[118] J. A. F.-L., II (1889), 102. Cf. vol. XIV (1901), 43 (Western Md.).
[119] J. A. F.-L., IV (1891), 267 f.
[120] J. A. F.-L., VII (1894), 116 f. For other cases, see vol. I (1888), 134 f; IV, 324 (Pa.).

testified that he had cut off and burned the ears of certain bewitched cattle, whereupon the defendant had come to his house "raging and scolding" and ceased only when the ears were taken out of the fire.[121] Today the Alleghany mountaineers cure bewitched cattle by cutting off and burning the tips of their ears and tails, bewitched horses by pressing on their foreheads a red-hot iron ring.[122] Butter and soft soap that will not 'come' are sometimes burned.[123] The spell of 'picking up tracks' can be counteracted only by fire.[124]

Persons suffering from "cunjer" are sometimes cured by the application of an outworn doctrine of primitive medicine which partakes of the nature of sympathetic magic. The underlying idea is that disease is attributable to the presence of evil spirits in the patient, and that, by transferring the demon to some other animal or to an inanimate object, the sufferer may be healed.[125] In many communities sick persons are passed through a split tree or some other aperture that they may be cured. According to an article in the *Southern Workman and Hampton School Quarterly* for 1896 (IX, 225), an American conjure-doctor once cured a bewitched person by sawing a tree in the middle and putting the patient through it.[126] Of the practice in Lincoln County a century ago,

---

[121] *Sadduc. Triumph.*, p. 327. The efficacy of the method is discussed in *An Advertisement to the Jury-Men of England*, edn. cit., p. 307.

[122] *J. A. F.-L.*, VII (1894), 115.

[123] *J. A. F.-L.*, XIV (1901), 43 (Western Md.). For other methods of injuring the witch by means of the conjured object, see *J. A. F.-L.*, II, 293 (N. H.); IV, 126 (Pa.); VI, 70 (Vt.).

[124] *J. A. F.-L.*, IX (1896), 228.

[125] Cf. W. G. Black, *Folk-Medicine*, p. 4 ff., and a recent article on "Demonology and Bacteriology in Medicine" in the *Scientific Monthly*. Lawson writes that in his day Indian doctors, or conjurers, told their people that "all Distempers are the effects of Evil Spirits, or the Bad Spirit which has struck them with this or that Malady." The author gives a detailed description of the Indian method of healing by driving out the "bad spirit." (*Op. cit.*, p. 126 f.). See further *Vergleichende Volksmedizin*, II (1909), 858 ff. For a collection of modern cases of nervous disorders attributed to demon possession, see Rev. J. L. Nevius, *Demon Possession and Allied Themes*, Revell, [1896?], p. 111 ff.

[126] See further Brand, *Pop. Antics.*, III (1901), 288 ff.; Black, *op. cit.*, p. 34 ff.; Cockayne, *Leechdoms*, I, liv. If a child is "liver-grown," take it "by the left leg and pass it three times around the leg of a table." (*Ill. Med. Journ.*, April, 1917, p. 270).

Mr. Coon writes: "The usual means resorted to to restore those who suffered from the spells worked by the hair balls thrown by witches was the following:

"The witch doctor would set a ladder up against a house, pass the patient from bottom to top and from top to bottom through the rungs, something like platting the 'splits' in the seat of a chair. After this performance, the patient was passed through a large horse collar, and a kind of magic oil or grease was used to make round rings on the patient's back. Dipping the thumbs of the patient in this oil ended the performance."

Here belong many cures for warts. For example, in western North Carolina a wart may be removed by cutting it until it bleeds, putting a drop of the blood on a grain of corn, and feeding the corn to a duck.[127] Another cure for warts, communicated to Mr.

---

[127] *J. A. F.-L.*, xx (1907), 249. Compare the cure for chills used by negroes in Maryland and Virginia (*J. A. F.-L.*, xxvi (1913), 190). See further the article on warts in the Boston *Herald* for December 16, 1907, and the methods recommended in *J. A. F.-L.*, vii (1894), 113; Black, *Folk-Medicine*, 185. This type of remedy was much used during the Middle Ages (cf. Cockayne, *Leechdoms*, i, xxx). In many communities, especially in Catholic countries, sick persons tie rags or parts of the clothing to the bushes surrounding wishing- or healing-wells, hoping by this operation to be freed of their ailments (cf. W. G. Wood-Martin, *Traces of the Elder Faiths of Ireland*, Longmans, ii (1902), 80 ff.). The belief that the evil spirit which causes the pain may be exorcised, explains the practice of "talking the fire" out of a burn. Mr. D. P. Smith writes that in eastern North Carolina certain especially gifted persons are still known as "fire-talkers" and that as a boy he was cured of a painful burn by an old lady who knew the magic formula. Mr. Coon asserts that, according to a belief formerly current in Lincoln County, the art of "talking out" fire could be taught to a woman only by a man, and vice versa. "The fire conjurer would hold one of his hands over the burn, repeat some words of enchantment, then remove the hand and blow the burn three times. If, for instance, the burn was on the hand, the blowing would be directed toward the ends of the fingers of the patient. If the burn was on the body, the blowing would be directed toward the nearest extremity. This performance was gone through with three times, each time the blowing was directed toward the nearest extremity and the hand of the conjurer moved over the wound in the direction of the extremity nearest the wound. The words were said in German, or 'Pennsylvania Dutch.' It was equivalent to losing the art for a conjurer of fire to reveal the enchanting words. These words were always said in a sing-song inaudible monotone that could not be understood by the bystanders." The formula used by a Devon-

Thomas Smith by John Dougherty, an uneducated farmer and blacksmith who has lived most of his life in the neighborhood of Zionville, runs as follows: "Take a little white flint rock for every wart you have, tie the flints up in a rag, then go to the nearest forks of the road; throw the rag with the flints over your shoulder into the road and walk off without looking back." Georgia negroes escape 'cunjer' ".by burying the cunjer bag in the public road where people walk"; thus the spell will lose its force by being divided.[128] Among Afro-Americans in general a bewitched person may injure the witch by burning the 'trick,' throwing it into the water, or returning it to the conjurer.[129]

Just as parts of the body may be used to produce conjure, so the spell may be removed by taking the parings of the toe and finger nails of the person bewitched and burying them at midnight at the foot of a white-oak tree.[130] In the same category belongs the following elaborate cure for bewitched children, said to have been in use a quarter of a century ago among the Alleghany mountains: "Measuring an infant, whose growth has been arrested, with an elastic cord that requires to be stretched in order to equal the child's length, will set it right again. If the spell be a wasting one, take three strings of similar or unlike colors, tie them to the front door or gate in such a manner that whenever either [is] opened there is some wear and tear on the cords. As use begins to tell on them, vigor will recommence."[131]

shire woman in healing a burn is quoted by Black (op. cit., p. 81, note). In Devonshire, as in North Carolina, the formula for curing a burn or scald should be communicated by a man to a woman, and vice versa (George Soane, *New Curiosities of Literature*, 2d. edn., London, I [1849], 205).

[128] *J. A. F.-L.*, XIV (1901), 177.

[129] *J. A. F.-L.*, IX (1896), 226.

[130] F. D. Bergen, *Animal and Plant Lore*, pp. 16, 102. In a seventeenth-century account given in Glanvill's *Sadduc. Triumph.*, (edn. cit., p. 334), a bewitched woman was relieved and the witch injured when some of the sufferer's urine, corked in a bottle with nails, pins, and needles, was buried in the ground.

[131] *J. A. F.-L.*, VII (1894), 116. Compare the "straining strings" used in connection with cures in Celtic communities (Wood-Martin, op. cit., II, 71 ff.). The colors of the strings are sometimes important; see F. T. Elworthy, op. cit., 58 f.; Black, *Folk-Medicine*, 108 ff. In Illinois the services of a "string-doctor" are still frequently in demand. In cases of

The American witch makes large use of small bundles or bags buried or otherwise hidden in or near the path of the intended victim (often under the doorstep of his house) and depending for their efficiency partly on sympathetic magic,[132] partly on vague reminiscences of primitive medical practice transmitted through generations of conjurers and quack doctors. It is here that African tradition appears to have been most influential on the technique of modern witchcraft in the South, [133] but no one can read many

erysipelas the "string-doctor" "passes a cord over the eruption, says a few magic words and the cord must be burned" (*Ill. Med. Journ.*, Apr., 1917, 269).

[132] The gradual rotting or rusting of the substances in the conjure-bag is accompanied by the wasting away of the victim (*J. A. F.-L.*, III [1890], 286). Cf. vol. XX, 160; X, 241.

[133] See the account of African negro charms given by Miss Kingsley, *Travels in West Africa*, London, 1897, p. 446 f.

The efficacy of "conjure" when properly placed and the methods used to counteract its effects are illustrated in a story told to Professor Benjamin Sledd, of Wake Forest College, by Sam Goff, a negro tenant on Professor Sledd's estate in Bedford County, Virginia. Sue, the wife of Ed Mayo, one of Sam's friends, suffered for two years from a mysterious ailment that prevented her from walking. At length, convinced that she had been bewitched by one Polly Ovaker, she dispatched her husband and Sam to Greenlea Ferry to ask the services of Jerry Ricketts, an albino, who had the reputation of being a powerful witch-doctor. Jerry, having assured himself that Sam and Ed believed in Witchcraft (without faith no cure could be effected), gave them a paper containing directions to be delivered to Sue, who fortunately could read. On returning to Ed's cabin, the two found Sue already partly recovered. On searching the premises in accordance with Jerry's instructions, they found a big-mouth black bottle containing a liquid hidden under the steps, and "a black gum-o'-'lastic ball 'bout big as a taw" buried in the sand at the bottom of the spring. Sue poured the liquid into a hole under "the big rock at the end o' the crossin'-log down at the creek"; the ball she placed in the fire. In each case her action was followed by an explosion. The witch soon appeared and attempted unsuccessfully to borrow provisions, and about sunset she tried to steal a lap-ful of chips. That night a big black cat entered Ed's cabin, but was driven off by the dogs, which later returned "lookin' used up an' slashed all about the nose an' years." Seeing nothing of the witch next day, Sam and others, overcome by curiosity, crept over to Polly's house the following night and peeped in. "All at once a light as blindin' as forked lightnin' flared up, right in the middle o' the cabin." Next morning all that remained of the place was a pile of ashes. Professor Sledd offers to have Sam repeat the story for any readers who happen to be skeptical.

accounts of the contents of negro "cunjer-bags" without being reminded of the ingredients of the witches' caldron in *Macbeth* or of the diabolical paraphernalia which Tam O'Shanter saw one stormy night through the windows of Kirk-Alloway. Witch charms of today apparently contain a large number of survivals of the materia medica of the Middle Ages. Substances which, when properly applied, are beneficent in their effects, may, when used by unblest hands, produce naught but evil. Strange drugs, many of animal origin, play an important part in primitive medicine.[134]

---

[134] Stones as amulets or cures are also widely used in folk-medicine. The society is indebted to Mr. D. P. Smith for the description of a "madstone." After recommending the madstone as a remedy for hydrophobia, the writer adds, "I will explain something about it, as I have seen one, and also seen one applied. There are only two or three in the world and they are in eastern North Carolina. It is a small stone about the size and shape of a piece of loaf sugar. It was originally used by the Indians and [from them] came to us. When placed near the wound, it sticks tightly . . . and often remains for several hours, at the end of which time the stone, that at first was a milky color, is a nasty greenish. . . . By soaking it in milk the stone recovers its natural color." In the autumn of 1917 the writer examined a madstone owned by Mr. J. B. Grimes, of Smithfield, Isle of Wight County, Virginia. The "stone" proved to be a small cube about 1/2" x 1/4" x 3/16", brownish on the larger surfaces, dark brown along the edges and on the ends. It looked like calcined bone or some porous wood, but Mr. Grimes was sure it was made of herbs. It was reported to have been made by one Seth Parker, of Cabin Point, Virginia. Accompanying the "stone" were the following printed instructions: "DIRECTIONS for using The Chinese Snake Stone. Scarify the wound before applying the Stone—take it off every morning and evening—put the Stone at each time, when taken off, into a glass of milk-warm water, and let it remain a few minutes, until it discharges itself of the poison—wash the wound in a strong solution of salt water, and scarify again, if necessary. After taking the Stone from the water, rub it dry in moderately warm ashes, and apply as before. This course should be repeated for the space of nine days, when a cure will be effected. The Stone must be applied to every wound. The patient must abstain from spirituous liquors. In case of fever, an occasional dose of salts will be found serviceable." Dr. Thomas M. Owen, Director of the Department of Archives and History of the State of Alabama, in a letter dated September 22, 1917, writes as follows: "After very extensive inquiry, I have located only one person who is said to make use of a madstone. His name and address is Dr. George M. Spencer, R. F. D., Greensboro, Ala." Accompanying the letter was a manuscript note on madstones from Dr. Owen's forthcoming *History of Alabama*. According to Dr. Owen, "some of these stones are reputed to have been

Dried reptiles, dried organs, excreta,[135] spiders,[136] ants, lizards, lobster claws, cat hair, and blood of deer, dove, rabbit, hog, or calf

taken from the stomach of a deer, but they were in fact nothing more than native rock, worn smooth, and which, because of their porosity, were capable when heated of drawing out, or absorbing liquids." The instructions given by Dr. Owen for using the madstone are much like those accompanying Mr. Grimes's specimen. (The *bezoar*, similar to the madstone in usage and frequently in composition, is a calcareous concretion found in the bodies of certain animals.) One of the writer's colleagues, who hails from Halifax County, Virginia, remembers having had a madstone applied to his own person when he was a boy. The stone resembled a fragment of ordinary whetstone. For further accounts of madstones or *bezoars* in Virginia, see Karl Knortz, *Zur amerikanischen Volkskunde*, p. 32 f. (Essex and Loudoun counties); *Denham Tracts*, II (1895), 233 f., (Richmond); James Thacker, *Observations on Hydrophobia*, Plymouth, Mass., 1812, p. 204 f. (Tappahannock); W. S. Walsh, *Handy Book of Curious Information*, Lippincott, 1913, p. 316 f. (Halifax Co.). For an account of madstones in the vicinity of Pulaski, Tennessee, consult *The Denham Tracts, loc. cit.*; for a *bezoar* taken from the stomach of a deer in the Chilhowee Mountains, see G. F. Kunz, *The Magic of Jewels and Charms*, Lippincott, 1915, p. 218. According to an early eighteenth-century report, *bezoars* were obtained from the bodies of deer in the Carolina mountains (Lawson, *op. cit.*, p. 72). For a wonderfully effective Kentucky madstone, see Black, *Folk-Medicine*, p. 144. Snakestones, used to cure snake-bite and popularly supposed to be formed by serpents, are often similar in composition to madstones and *bezoars*. On these and similar objects used from remote antiquity to heal the bites of serpents and dogs, see G. F. Kunz, *The Curious Lore of Precious Stones*, Lippincott, 1913, p. 367 ff.; E. N. Santini de Riolo, *Les pierres magiques*, Paris, 1905, p. 34 f.; Walter Johnson, *Folk Memory*, Oxford, 1908, p. 121 ff.; *Proc. Am. Phil. Soc.*, XXVI (1889), 337, note; Geo. H. Bratley, *The Power of Gems and Charms*, London, 1907, p. 103 f.; *Orphei lithica*, ed., E. Abel, Berolini, 1881, p. 157 f.; W. G. Wood-Martin, *Traces of the Elder Faiths of Ireland*, Longmans, II (1902), 67 ff.; *N. & Q.*, 9th Ser., VI, 477; VII, 12, 135, 335; Brand, *Pop. Antiqs.*, III (1901), 295; Eugene Tavenner, *Studies in Magic from Latin Lit.*, New York, 1916, p. 9, n. 40. For several of the references given above the writer is indebted to Professor Kittredge.

[135] Scot, *op. cit.*, p. 63.

[136] On the bad reputation of the spider, see Kittredge, *The Old Farmer*, p. 104 ff. Dr. Brickell describes the symptoms of poisoning by spiders and prescribes an early eighteenth-century cure. His book recommends a number of medicaments composed of insects (*Natural History of North Carolina*, edn. cit., 159 ff.). On fleas and lice in folk-lore, see Karl Knortz, *Die Insekten in Sage, Sitte u. Literatur*, Annaberg (Sachsen), 1910, p. 47 ff.

were all anciently used for medical purposes.[137] In the United States reptiles,[138] animal matter of various kinds (including hair,[139] viscera, and urine [140]), red pepper,[141] assafœtida,[142] the powder contained in a large mushroom called the "devil's snuff-box,[143] a plant known as the "king-root," [144] pokeberry root,[145] and other

[137] See R. H. True, "Folk Materia Medica" (*J. A. F.-L.*, XIV [1901], 105 ff.); Black, *op. cit..* p. 148 ff.; J. M. Beveridge, "Survivals of Superstition as Found in the Practice of Medicine" (*Ill. Med. Journ.*, April, 1917, p 267 ff.); T. A. Wise, *Commentary on the Hindu System of Medicine*, Calcutta, 1845, p. 114 ff. In 1889 it was reported among the colored population of South Carolina that doctors made castor oil out of negroes' blood (*J. A. F.-L.*, III (1890), 285). The Boston *Post* for March 24th, 1908, announces the death of Mary Jane Fleming, the "veiled lady" of 80 Harvard Street, Cambridge, who made her living "by selling hand-made flatiron holders and 'conjure charms' such as dried birds' heads, 'black cat gizzards,' so called, and rabbits' feet." There was a rumor that the woman was a negress. In Georgia and South Carolina the hair-ball found in the stomach of a cow produces conjure and counteracts witchcraft (*J. A. F.-L.*, III (1890), 286). In the early eighteenth century the Indian conjurers of eastern North Carolina were skilled in the use of herbs; they were credited with marvellous cures and were charged with wholesale poisoning (Lawson, *op. cit.*, pp. 129 f., 134).

[138] Dr. Brickell gives prescriptions for various remedies of reptilian origin (*op. cit.*, pp. 77, 141, 147). According to Mr. D. P. Smith, it is still a popular belief in eastern North Carolina that a live toad-frog cut in two and applied to the bite of a mad dog, will draw out the venom. During the early eighteenth century Indian children who persisted in eating dirt were forced to partake of a bat skinned and roasted (Lawson, *op. cit.*, p. 73).

[139] Cf. F. D. Bergen, *Animal and Plant Lore*, p. 71 f., Karl Knortz, *Reptilien u. Amphibien*, p. 63.

[140] *J. A. F.-L.*, XVI (1903), 68; XVII, 36, 107. Cf. vol. XIV, 177.

[141] *J. A. F.-L.*, XIV (1901), 175 (Ga.-negro). In the sixteenth century sage was used in witch charms (Scot, *op. cit.*, p. 47).

[142] To prevent horses from being bewitched, rub with lard or assafœtida (*J. A. F.-L.*, VII [1894] 114; Alleghany Mountains). Among the negroes of South Carolina assafœtida worn around the neck is an antidote for witch spells (*J. A. F.-L.*, IX, 129 f.). Cf. vol. XVII, 126; XXVII, 246 (S. C.); XIV, 39 (Md.). On the use of brimstone to prevent conjure, see *So. Workman*, XLI (1912), 248.

[143] *J. A. F.-L.*, XIV (1901), 177 f. (Ga.-negro). See also *So. Workman*, XXIX (1900), 180.

[144] *J. A. F.-L.*, XII (1899), 229. Cf. vol. IX, 145.

[145] *J. A. F.-L.*, XIV (1901), 177 (Ga.-negro).

herbs [146] enter into the practice of witchcraft or of popular medicine. Among the mountain whites of the Alleghanies "maidenhair" mixed with the fodder will make bewitched cattle give milk.[147] The use of saliva is notorious.[148] In the mountains of North Carolina, making a cross and spitting in it is a familiar charm against the baneful influences of black cats and graveyard rabbits.[149] Mr. D. P. Smith, who has been good enough to record some traditions for the society, asserts that conjure-bags are still used by witches in eastern North Carolina, and relates that on a visit to a witch's cabin, he found the walls decorated with "such things as drying roots and plants, snake skins, dried frogs, [and] cow's horns." In Georgia conjure-doctors use the heads of snakes and "scorpions" in whiskey,[150] as well as any or all of the following assortment: earthworms, snake-skins, leaves or sticks tied with horse-hair, black owl's feathers, wings of bats, tails of rats, and feet of moles.[151] A Georgia negro found under his door-step a "cunjer-bag" containing "small roots about an inch long, some black hair, a piece of snake skin, and some yaller graveyard dirt, dark yaller, right off some coffin."[152] The number of effective combinations appears to be very large, but the following from Morotuck, Virginia, is recommended as especially powerful: "Take a bunch of hair or wool, a rabbit's paw, and a chicken gizzard, tie them up in a cotton rag and fasten the bundle to some implement which the man to be injured is in the habit of using."[153]

The ancient belief that the influence of the moon, now recognized as determining the tides, extends over all animal and vegetable life, accounts for the fact that Georgia witches, like the weird sisters in *Macbeth*, gather their herbs during certain phases of the moon.

[146] Cf. *J. A. F.-L.*, v (1892), 182 (Pa.).
[147] *J. A. F.-L.*, VII (1894), 114.
[148] Cf. Black, *op. cit.*, p. 184; *Pop. Sci. Mo.*, XXXIX (1891), 373 f. "If your right hand itches, spit in it and rub it in your pocket; you are going to get some money" (*So. Workman*, XLI (1912), 248).
[149] F. D. Bergen, *Animal and Plant Lore*, p. 17; *J. A. F.-L.*, XX (1907), 246 (N. C.).
[150] *So. Workman*, XXIX (1900), 443.
[151] *J. A. F.-L.*, XIV (1901), 178.
[152] *J. A. F.-L.*, XIII (1900), 228.
[153] *J. A. F.-L.*, X (1899), 241. For other combinations, see *J. A. F.-L.*, III, 206 (Ga.), 282 (Ala.); VII, 154 (Va.); XII, 289; XIII, 212 (La.); *Century Mag.*, XXI (1885-86), 820.

In some districts it is also held that "cunjer" should be laid down on the increase of the moon, so that it will "rise up and grow."[154]

[154] *J. A. F.-L.*, XIII (1900), 228. Among the folk the phases of the moon are important for the success of many operations. In western North Carolina "all plants which produce fruit above ground must be planted in the light of the moon, not necessarily in a new moon; and all plants which produce fruit underground, potatoes and such, must be planted in the dark of the moon. Also the hogs must be killed in the dark of the moon, or the bacon and lard will shrink" (*J. A. F.-L.*, XX (1907), 242). Plant seeds, make soap, kill meat, and wash and dye warp on the increase of the moon; otherwise your labor will be in vain. For evidence, see *J. A. F.-L.*, VI (1893), 299 (Tenn.); VII, 305; XII, 265 (Ga.); X, 77 (Western Canada); X, 214 (Newfoundland); XII, 133 (Southern Highlands); XXVI, 190 (Va. and Md.); XXVII, 245 (S. C.); F. D. Bergen, *Current Superstitions*, 1896, 120 f. (Ala.), 157 (Pa.); Gummere, *op. cit.*, 59 (Pa); and Kittredge, *The Old Farmer*, 305 f. (N. E.). Do not lay shingles in the dark of the moon (*J. A. F.-L.*, XXVII, 245: S. C.). See further the Chicago *Tribune* for May 4th, 1915, p. 1; *The Folk-Lorist* (Journal of the Chicago Folk-Lore Soc.), I (1892), p. 56; *Popular Treatises on Science Written during the Middle Ages*, ed., Thomas Wright, London, 1841, p. 15. In the Cumberland Mountains a "fence worm" laid in the dark of the moon will sink into the ground (E. B. Miles, *The Spirit of the Mountains*, 106). An Old English astrological tract asserts that timber felled at the full moon will resist decay longest (Cockayne, *Leechdoms*, III, 269). Cf. Soane, *New Curiosities of Lit.*, p. 146. The following from Lincoln county, N. C., are communicated by Mr. Coon: "You should always plant potatoes in the dark of the moon, between new moon and full moon, so that the hills will be full. ... You should plant onions when the point of the moon is turned downwards, so that the onions may grow large and not be all tops and seeds. ... In order that corn may ear well near the ground and not grow so tall, it must be planted when the little moon is turned down and on to the time when it is new. .... If you wish the color to be fast, the coloring should be done in the light of the moon, especially if a good fast blue [is] desired. ... Every one should cut pine timber in the new moon and oak timber in the dark of the moon. Pine timber cut in the light of the moon will season well; in the dark of the moon it will be soggy. Boards should be put on the roof 'in the little moon down,' to keep them [from] turning up toward the sun. .... Hogs should be killed from the 'new to full moon' in order to keep the meat from 'cooking away' and in order that it [may] 'season' well. Manure should be put on the fields between the new moon and the first quarter. If put on the field in the light of the moon, it would do little good. ... Wheat should be ground in the dark of the moon in October, so that bugs and worms [will] remain clear of the flour and it [will] remain good for twelve months." On the importance of the moon in popular medicine, see Black, *op. cit.*, pp. 124 ff., 151. In the *Ill. Med. Journ.* for April, 1917, p. 270,

The practice of witchcraft and of popular medicine in the United States still preserves traces of an ancient and wide-spread superstition which attributes magic properties to the human hand.[155] Healing by the laying on of hands (familiar in the custom of touching for the King's Evil) or by contact with the hand of a corpse, depends ultimately on the belief that the mysterious powers of the human hand especially fit it for transferring disease. Dr.

Dr. Beveridge writes, "I have been asked the time of the moon to wean a baby and have been compelled to confess my ignorance. A family once delayed a tonsillectomy. The father explained later that they waited for the dark of the moon to lessen hemorrhage." According to Dr. G. H. Macon, some North Carolina midwives still predict the date of their patients' delivery by the phases of the moon (*Trans. Med. Soc. of N. C.*, Raleigh, 1918, p. 217).

It would be interesting to discover what traditions persist in North Carolina regarding the Man of the Signs, or the Moon's Man, the figure of a man surrounded by the twelve signs of the Zodiac which is still to be seen in many almanacks in circulation throughout the country districts. I think I have heard that in Orange County it is regarded as dangerous to castrate hogs except "when the signs are in the feet." Mr. Coon records several rules formerly observed in Lincoln County. Beans should be planted "in the sign of the 'scales,' so that the stalks will be weighted with beans." Cotton seed should also be planted "in the sign of the 'scales,' so that the cotton will weigh heavily." Cucumber seeds should be sowed in the sign of the 'twins,' "so that the vines may produce twice as many cucumbers as otherwise." "Cabbage seed should be sowed in the sign of the 'head' for obvious reasons." "Calves should be weaned in the sign of the fishes. At that time they will soon forget their mothers. If calves [are] weaned in the sign of the feet, they [will] not bawl and lament the loss of their mothers. Calves ought never to be weaned in the sign of the head." According to the *Kalendar of Shepherdes*, an early sixteenth-century English translation of a French compendium of scientific lore, "a man ought not to make incysyon ne touche with yren ye membre gouerned of any sygne the day that the mone is in it for fere of to grete effusyon of blode that myght happen, ne in lykewyse also when the sonne is in it, for the daunger & peryll that myght ensue." (Quoted by Kittredge, *The Old Farmer*, p. 53). Dr. J. M. Beveridge (*Ill. Med. Journ.*, Apr., 1917, p. 270) is authority for the following: "A Minnesota doctor writes me that a woman would not allow an operation on her child till the sign of the zodiac pointed to the part of the body requiring the operation. . . . I know a doctor who kept a record of the sign of the zodiac in which his obstetric cases occurred."

[155] On the general subject of the arm, hand, and finger in popular lore, see Karl Knortz, *Der menschliche Körper in Sage, Brauch u. Sprichwort*, Würzburg, 1909, p. 141 ff.; *Vergleichende Volksmedizin*, II (1909), 877.

Frank Baker, in a paper read on May 4, 1886, before the Anthropological Society of Washington (D. C.), mentions a number of recent instances in which persons touched the hands of corpses in order to be healed of various disorders.[156] Among the mountain whites of the South witch-doctors still cure certain ailments by gently rubbing the part affected, at the same time repeating a meaningless formula.[157] "If a rapid cure is to be effected, interrupted pressure must be made with a hand in which a mole has been squeezed to death."[158] Alabama negroes believe that one of the ways to cure toothache is to place in the mouth the finger of a corpse.[159] A voodoo charm from Louisiana includes, along with a lock of hair from a dead natural child, a powder made of "the little finger of a person who committed suicide" and other ingredients, all to be wrapped in a piece of a shroud and placed under the victim's pillow.[160] Mrs. Fanny D. Bergen, in her book on *Animal and Plant Lore* (p. 78) asserts that in southern Georgia negroes still believe in the "hand of glory" (*main de gloire*)[161]—a gruesome appliance consisting of a human hand cut from the corpse of

[156] The paper appeared under the title, "Anthropological Notes on the Human Hand," in the *American Anthoropologist*, I (1888), 51 ff. See further F. D. Bergen, *Current Superstition*, 131 f.; Black, *Folk-Medicine*, pp. 100 ff., 176; Karl Knortz, *Zur amerikanischen Volkskunde*, p. 30.

[157] A wizard who described his method of procedure to Mr. James Mooney, said that he rubbed the patient until he felt the disease enter at the tips of his fingers, then mount gradually to his arms, and so pass into his body. At first he could shake off the disease current from his fingers as one shakes drops of water from the hand, but as it became stronger it filled his whole body. When the sensation became unendurable, he rushed to the nearest stream and washed the contagion away. "According to his own statement," says Mr. Mooney, "the ordeal always left him in an exhausted condition, and it seemed as if he himself really had faith in the operation." *J. A. F.-L.*, II (1889), p. 102. Is it still believed anywhere in North Carolina that murder can be detected by the bleeding of the corpse at the touch of the guilty person? On the "ordeal by touch" in New England, see Kittredge, *The Old Farmer*, 74 ff.

[158] *J. A. F.-L.*, VII (1894), 111 f. Cf. IV, 326 (Pa.).

[159] *So. Workman*, XXIX (1900), 443.

[160] *J. A. F.-L.*, XIII (1900), 212. Compare the use of human bones by Georgia negroes as talismans against witchcraft (*J. A. F.-L.*, XIV, 178).

[161] The name is a deformation by popular etymology of the Old French *mandegore*, originally *mandragore*, the mandrake, the root of which was anciently used for narcotic, aphrodisiac, and magical purposes. (*N. E. D.*, s. v. "hand of glory.") Cf. *Vergl. Volksmedizin*, I (1908), 16 ff.

a criminal and used as a candlestick by malefactors during the Middle Ages.[162] According to popular belief the "hand of glory" casts into a stupor those in whose presence it is lighted. The subject has found literary treatment in Harrison Ainsworth's *Rookwood*, Scott's *Antiquary* (chap. xvii), Barham's *Ingoldsby Legends* (The Nurse's Story), and Southey's *Thalaba* (bk. v).[163] A generation ago, says Dr. Baker, "detached portions of the dead hand were quite commonly used among the illiterate classes for some supposed lucky influence that they bring." As lately as the winter of 1885-6 a janitor in the Georgetown Medical College stole from the dissecting room a human hand, which he later presented to his paramour, a dissolute Southern woman of the poorer class. The woman said she expected to use the gift "for luck and to find money and treasure with." [164]

[162] The candles generally contained as one of their ingredients grease distilled from corpses. Cf. Black, *Folk-Medicine*, 98; St. John D. Seymour, *Irish Witchcraft and Demonology*, 27; Grimm, *Deut. Mythol.*, II, 898, n. 1. Qy.: have witches in the South ever been charged with digging up bodies for purposes of sorcery? The practise was legislated against under James I (Kittredge, *Proc. Am. Ant. Soc.*, XVIII (1907), 7, n. 4). Cf. Dalton, *op. cit.*, p. 276. The statute is quoted by Ashton, *op. cit.*, p. 137 f. During the great period of witchcraft prosecutions in Western Europe witches were accused of sacrificing their children to the devil (Scot, *op. cit.*, p. 25), of eating human flesh (*op. cit.*, p. 26), and of boiling corpses to make grease "whereby they ride in the aire" (*op. cit.*, p. 32). In 1590 a Scottish witch confessed that she and other persons had been commanded by the devil to dig up three dead bodies and use parts of them "to make a powder . . . to do evil with" (*Sadduc. Triumph.*, p. 399). The voodoo doctors of the West Indies, especially Haiti, have often been charged with murdering infants for purposes of witchcraft. (See *Am. Anthrop.*, I (1888), 288 f.; H. Prichard, *Where Black Rules White*, N. Y., 1900, 74 ff.; *So. Workman*, XXXVI, 401 ff.; *Folk-Lore*, XXVI (1915), 255. The *New York World Magazine* for September 20th, 1908, contains an account of how during August of the same year a negro in Havana, Cuba, stole a white child for the purpose of procuring its heart and blood, "which had been prescribed by witches as medicine for his mother." On the general subject of voodoo, see F. D. Bergen, *Animal and Plant Lore*, p. 126 f. It is said that apothecaries still receive inquiries for human oil to be used for medicinal purposes (Karl Knortz, *Zur amerikanischen Volkskunde*, p. 24).

[163] See also H. M. Rideout's story in the *Sat. Eve. Post* for June 26th, 1915.

[164] Mr. T. J. Westropp (*Lolk-Lore*, XXII (1911), 340) reports a recent "case of stirring (bewitched) butter with a dried human hand" in order to make it come. The events are said to have taken place in Ireland.

An extension of the same general belief makes it lucky to carry the forepaw of an animal. A rabbit's foot carried about the person is a well-known talisman to insure good luck. A recent communication to the North Carolina Folk-Lore Society recommends the right hind foot, but the more common opinion seems to be that the left hind foot has the greater power. The rabbit should be one that frequents a graveyard,[165] or should be caught under a gallows. If the charm is to be most effective, the foot should be cut from the living animal, the rabbit should be released, and the foot should then be dipped (three times?) in "stump-water" (at midnight?)[166] In 1886 the poor whites of North Carolina believed that a mole's paw, cut from the living animal, was especially efficacious in bringing good luck,[167] and today in North Carolina a child who wears a mole's paw around its neck will not be sick while teething.

Witches have long been accused of eating corpses or of using them otherwise in their profession. A shocking negro story from Guilford County, North Carolina, tells of a woman who refused to eat with her husband and who was subsequently discovered to be a devourer of dead bodies. At night, when her husband was asleep, "she would slip out . . . an' go out to de graveyards. An' one day, when they had a buryin', he decided to watch her. That night, when she got up an' got dressed an' went out, he dressed an' went out behin'. He hid behin' a bush. She would dig up that body an' cut off slashes of 'em jus' like meat, an' eat 'em." Thereupon the husband slipped quietly back to bed. When

---

[165] F. D. Bergen, *Animal and Plant Lore*, p. 12. Cf. *J. A. F.-L.*, XII (1899), 261 (Ga.). According to certain classical authorities whose works found their way into Old English, parts of some animals used as cures are effective only when cut from the living body (Cockayne, *Leechdoms*, I, pp. xvi, xviii, xxix, 327 f.). A communication from eastern North Carolina recommends a live frog cut in half and applied to the wound as a cure for the bite of a mad dog. For pains in the joints an English prescription directs that a toad be tied belly downwards on the affected part (Richard Blakeborough, *Wit, Character, Folklore and Customs of the North Riding of Yorkshire*, Saltburn-by-the-Sea, 1911, p. 130). According to a belief still prevalent in some parts of Illinois thrush may be cured by placing a live minnow or small frog in the mouth of the patient (*Ill. Med. Journ.*, Apr., 1917, 269).

[166] Cf. *J. A. F.-L.*, II (1889), 100.

[167] *Am. Anthrop.*, I, 54.

accused of her action, the woman beat her husband severely and disappeared. "An' she was gone, an' never was foun' any mo'."[168] In one of the Lancashire trials of 1612 a witness told the court that she had seen two witches dig up the body of a child and afterwards cook and eat it.[169]

Though the use of corpses is less common in modern than in ancient witchcraft, witches of the present day, especially among the negroes of the South, have great faith in the baneful effects of "graveyard dirt." According to a negro superstition current in Georgia, the soil, to be effective, must be taken from the grave one day after the funeral.[170] It is, however, carefully guarded by the "hants," and even witch-doctors can get it only by the use of charms.[171] When placed on the ground, it has the peculiar property of working its way down to the same depth as the lid of the coffin from which it was taken. A Georgia negro who had been made ill by graveyard dirt placed under his house, took out as much as he could get at and burned it; but some he couldn't reach, as it kept sinking into the ground.[172]

The elf-shot, so deadly to man and beast during the Middle Ages, finds a close parallel in the missiles used by the modern witch.[173] Among the white population of the Alleghany Mountains witches kill cattle by shooting them with balls of hair,[174] and in western Maryland "witches' bullets" of pith or hair are often found in the bodies of dead animals.[175] Mr. Coon reports that a century

---

[168] *J. A. F.-L.*, XXX, 187. In three other stories from Guilford County a mother kills and cooks her child (*Ibid.*, 196 f.).

[169] Wright, *Narratives*, II, 129.

[170] *J. A. F.-L.*, XIV (1901), 180. Cf. Black, *Folk-Medicine*, 95 ff. In England certain plants used in the preparation of home-made remedies, should be gathered from a grave (E. M. Wright, *Rustic Speech and Folk-Lore*, Ox. Univ. Press, 1913, p. 235).

[171] *J. A. F.-L.*, XIII (1900), 228.

[172] *J. A. F.-L.*, XIV (1901), 176; cf. III (1890), 284 f. According to an ante-bellum tradition from Alabama, dogs cannot track you if you put graveyard dirt in your shoes (*So. Workman*, XXXIII (1904), 52).

[173] In country districts of the British Isles prehistoric flint weapons are believed to be elf-shots, and water into which a stone celt or arrow-head has been dipped, is used as a remedy for elf-shotten cattle or persons. Cf. E. M. Wright, *Rustic Speech*, 235; Wood-Martin, *Traces of the Elder Faiths*, I, p. 41 f.

[174] *J A. F.-L.*, VII (1894), 114. Cf. Glanvill, *Sadduc. Triumph.*, 398.

[175] *J. A. F.-L.*, XIV (1901), 42.

ago in Lincoln County, North Carolina, witches shot their missiles mostly by night and that "the slightest touch of the breath of those swift flying balls resulted in loss of youth and physical strength." According to an ancient belief worms in men and beasts are elfish demons,[176] and it is well known that modern witches can "throw" lizards and other vermin into the bodies of their victims. A mixture used by witches in Georgia consists of dried snakes, "scorpions," "ground-puppies," and "toad-frogs" reduced to a powder. When this preparation is taken internally, the "varmints" come to life and devour the body.[177] In one case a conjure-doctor, employed to remove a spell of this kind, took from a man's leg a lizard and a grasshopper.[178]

A considerable number of witch-spells and counter-charms are justified by the wide-spread popular belief that reversal in process involves reversal in result; if doing a thing one way works good, doing it the opposite way produces evil. Thus Christian symbols and formulae, so often employed against witchcraft,[179] are used in

---

[176] Grimm, Deut. Mythol., II, 965 f. Cf. J. A. F.-L., XXII (1909), 217. During the sixteenth and seventeenth centuries bewitched persons sometimes vomited pins, needles, wool, straw, cotton yarn, feathers, and even buttons. For instances, see Scot, Disc. of Witchcraft, p. 106; Glanvill, Sadduc. Triumph., p. 315; Wright, Narratives, II, 133. According to Dalton (op. cit., p. 278), such vomiting is an evidence of being bewitched.

[177] J. A. F.-L., XIV (1901), 180. The following note, hitherto unpublished, is found in the Bodleian manuscript, Gough Ireland 3 (p. 25b), which contains "Notes of remarkable occurrences in Ireland, from about 1731 to 1753, and of some curiosities there, by Edward Steele": "On the last Friday in April 1747, Mary Saunders, of Stronkelly, in the Barony of Coshbridge, in the County of Waterford, made Oath before William Smith of Hedborough, Esq; Justice of the Peace for that County, that she threw out of her Stomach, in Consequence of some Remedies, particularly a Vomit given her by Dominick Sarsefield, Esq; Doctor of Physick of Cork, a four footed Creature, about four Inches long, and one broad, dead, of a black Colour, resembling a small Water Rat, or Weasel, which she produced to him."

[178] J. A. F.-L., XIII (1900), 228 (Ga.-negro). A lame man in Chestertown, Md., said a snake had been conjured into his leg (J. A. F.-L., III (1890), 285). An Atlanta (Ga.) negro was terrified because he believed his vitals had been set on fire (J. A. F.-L., III, 281). Cf. J. A. F.-L., I, 83; V, 123 (Ark.); IX, 225 f.

[179] The sign of the cross is, of course, a familiar means of averting evil. See F. D. Bergen, Animal and Plant Lore, p. 17; J. A. F.-L., XX (1907), 246; and p. 267, n. 149, above. For other uses of the cross in Christian

reverse order by the witches themselves. For example, in Alabama witches conjure by saying the Lord's Prayer backwards.[180]. On the Eastern Shore of Maryland reading the Bible forwards, very properly prevents injury from ghosts after they have got into the house, but, strange to say, reading it backwards prevents them from

formulae and in charms against witchcraft, see *J. A. F.-L.*, IV, 324 f.; XVII, 127 f. (Pa.); XIV, 178 (Ga.). If you sleep with a bible under your head, witches will not disturb you (*J. A. F.-L.*, IX, 129 f.: S. C.-negro). Among the mountain whites of the Alleghanies a bible is used by witch-doctors in discovering thieves (*J. A. F.-L.*, VII, 113). In the sixteenth and seventeenth centuries persons suspected of witchcraft were sometimes weighed against a bible. For an American case, see *J. A. F.-L.*, V, 149 f.; (cf. II, 32) but contrast Gummere, *op. cit.*, p. 55. Occasionally quacks or ignorant dabblers in the black art use Christian words and symbols in their practice. For cases in point, see *J. A. F.-L.*, I (1888), 138 f.; III, 284 f.; Black, *Folk-Medicine*, p. 83. Compare the crossed feathers in the voodoo charm described in the *Century Mag.*, XXI, 820. For an early instance, see *Sadduc. Triumph.*, 398. Lawson saw an Indian conjurer use the sign of the cross (*op. cit.*, p. 129).

[180] F. D. Bergen, *Animal and Plant Lore*, 127. Reciting a verse of Scripture backwards forms part of a charm for summoning Satan given in the *J. A. F.-L.*, XXV (1912), 134. According to an English belief current during the seventeenth century, a witch cannot say the Lord's Prayer (*Sadduc. Triumph.*, 317). Cf. E. L. Linton, *Witch Stories*, London, 1861, p. 381.

Cabalistic signs, abracadabra, and scraps of foreign languages, especially Latin and Greek, have long been used by dabblers in magic. A corruption of the well-known word-square,

```
S A T O R
A R E P O
T E N E T
O P E R A
R O T A S
```

is said to have been in use not long since among the witch-doctors of the Alleghany Mountains (*J. A. F.-L.*, VII (1894), 113). The form communicated to Mr. Porter by a mountain conjurer omits the word OPERA. The formula is correctly given in "The Long Hidden Friend" (*J. A. F.-L.*, XVII, 127), a reprint of a vulgar treatise on occult lore long current in German Pennsylvania, and in the dissertation on Anglo-Saxon charms published in the same journal (XXII, 113). See further F. T. Elworthy; *The Evil Eye*, 401, where it is said to be used with the Lord's Prayer to heal the bite of a mad dog. On magic writings as remedies, see Black, *Folk-Medicine*, p. 165 ff.

entering.[181] The negroes of central Georgia say that if a rabbit crosses the road ahead of you, you should not only cross yourself, at the same time making a cross on the ground and spitting in it, but also walk backwards over the spot where the rabbit's path intersects your own.[182] A similar tradition prevails among the negroes of Virginia and Maryland.[183] Unless soft soap and baking mixtures are stirred continually in the same direction, they will not be successful. It may be added that the direction, even when not indicated (as in a case from North Carolina),[184] is probably not a matter of indifference.[185] In versions of the superstition current in several other states the proper direction is "with the sun"[186]—perhaps a survival of the dextral, or sunwise, circuit so common in certain savage rites.

In some cases merely turning an article of clothing inside out serves to avert the witch's spell, the popular notion apparently being that the changed appearance prevents the witch from recognizing her victim. In western North Carolina those disturbed by nightmare drive away the troublesome visitor by getting out of bed and turning their shoes over.[187] It is a matter of common knowledge that turning the stockings inside out before retiring prevents disturbance from witches. In central Georgia negroes keep away spirits and witches by wearing their coats inside out.[188]

[181] *J. A. F.-L.*, II (1889), 298, n. 2. Cf. F. D. Bergen, *Animal and Plant Lore*, p. 15.

[182] *J. A. F.-L.*, XII (1899), 262. Cf. *So. Workman*, XLI (1912), 246.

[183] *J. A. F.-L.*, XXVI (1913), 190.

[184] *J. A. F.-L.*, XX (1907), 243.

[185] Scot (*Disc. of Witchcraft*, p. 163) quotes Plutarch to the effect that the unlucky side from which to receive an augury, is the right, "because terrene and mortall things are opposite & contrarie to divine and heavenlie things, for that which the gods deliver with the right hand, falleth to our left side; and so contrariwise."

[186] F. D. Bergen, "Survivals of Sun-Worship," *Pop. Sci. Mo.*, XLVII (1895), 249 ff.; *Current Superstitions*, pp. 123, 158 f.

[187] *J. A. F.-L.*, V (1892), 115. In the vicinity of Zionville, North Carolina, putting on a garment wrong side out in the morning is regarded as a portent of ill luck for the day. If a woman unwittingly puts on her dress inside out, she will have good luck inside of twelve hours (Karl Knortz, *Zur amerikanischen Volkskunde*, Tübingen, 1905, p. 5). So in some sections of the Carolina mountains (*J. A. F.-L.*, II, 101).

[188] *J. A. F.-L.*, XII (1899), 261. Cf. XVII, 108 (Pa.). To stop a screech-owl from hollo'ing, turn the pocket inside out (*So. Workman*, XXXIII [1904], 51; F. D. Bergen, *Animal and Plant Lore*, p. 20: Ala.-negro); or

The story of Phoebe Ward, given above, illustrates one of the witch's oldest and most firmly established powers. Like the *striga* of classical tradition and the Raging Host of Germanic folk-lore, the modern hag can fly through the air.[189] That the power of levitation was also attributed to the Indian medicine-men of North Carolina during the early eighteenth century, is shown by the following statement made by Lawson on the authority of eye-witnesses: "They [the witnesses] have seen [a Chowan conjurer] take a reed about two foot long in his mouth, and stand by a Creek-Side, where he called twice or thrice with the Reed in his mouth, and at last, has opened his Arms and fleed over the Creek, which might be near a quarter of a Mile wide or more."[190] From the data at hand it appears that in the South, at least among the negro population, the familiar tradition that witches ride broom-sticks on their midnight excursions, exists more as a sophisticated than as a genuinely popular superstition.[191] The witch's mount is most frequently an animal—either a beast *sans phrase* or a transformed human being.[192] As Mr. Stephenson's story shows, the witch's flight is facilitated by the utterance of a magic formula[193] and is

turn the pockets and set the shoes upside down (*J. A. F.-L.*, VII (1894), 305: Ga.). On superstitions connected with turning the garments, see further Karl Knortz, *Amerikanischer Aberglaube der Gegenwart*, p. 25.

[189] For other recent instances, see *J. A. F.-L.*, II (1889), 292 (N. H.); X, 240 f.; XII, 68 (Md.-negro); XIV, 40; XXVII, 306 f. (N. Y.). For earlier evidence, see Grimm, *Deut. Mythol.*, II, 878 f. Cf. Thomas Ady, *A Candle in the Dark*, London, 1656, 108; *Remains Historical and Literary of the Palatine Counties of Lancaster and Chester* (Chetham Soc.), 1845; *passim*; *The Witches of Northamptonshire*, London, 1612 (in a collection of reprints of early tracts in the Harvard College Library).

[190] *Op. cit.*, p. 129. Cf. Brickell, *op. cit.*, p. 375. For another Indian story involving levitation, see *Am. Anthrop.*, N. S. II (1909), 269 ff.

[191] In 1663 a woman named Julian Cox, tried in Somersetshire (England), said that she had once met three witches "upon three Broom-staves, born up about a yard and a half from the ground" (*Sadduc. Triump.*, p. 323). A woman tried for witchcraft in Pennsylvania in 1683, confessed that she had ridden through the air on a broomstick (Gummere, *op. cit.*, p. 39). In the sixteenth century witches were said to dance at their sabbaths with brooms held aloft in their hands (Scot, *Disc. of Witchcraft*, p. 32 f.).

[192] See below, p. 281, and the western Maryland story, *J. A. F.-L.*, XIV (1901), 40 f.

[193] In 1664 the English witch Elizabeth Style confessed that while passing through the air, she and her confederates repeated a rigmarole somewhat like Phœbe Ward's rhyme (*Sadduc. Triumph.*, p. 297).

brought to a disastrous conclusion if she speaks while crossing a stream [194] — a fact which suggests the old belief about spirits' inability to cross running water and the well recognized power of the spoken word to counteract magic.

The popular fear of witches on their nocturnal peregrinations is greatly enhanced by the fact that these night-flying terrors can enter a house through any small aperture such as a keyhole.[195] The royal author of *Daemonologie* asserts that during the late sixteenth century witches believed themselves capable of 'piercing through whatsoeuer open the aire may enter in at,'[196] and the accusation against the Virginia witch Grace Sherwood in 1698 that she had escaped from Anthony Barnes's house through "the Key hole or crack of the door,"[197] is paralleled by similar charges brought against English and Continental witches during the two preceding centuries.[198] In a story from North Carolina received some years ago, a witch succeeded in getting into a house by uttering the words, "Through the key-hole I go!" and in another account from the same district a witch's daughter who had been carried by her mother into a neighbor's house, broke the charm by speaking and was thus unable to escape.[199] The unwelcome visitor may also be captured if the hole is stopped, since "for witches this is law: where they have entered, there also they withdraw." This principle furnishes the rationale of a large group of stories in which witches are confused with swan-maidens and other captured fairy women, familiar in European folk-lore. The following is typical and should find parallels in North Carolina. A miller in Frederick County, Maryland, who was troubled with nightmare, decided that his nocturnal visitor was a witch and accordingly one night stopped the keyhole of his room. Next morning he found a beautiful girl cowering in the cupboard. After keeping the

---

[194] Compare the fate of the young man who spoke while riding a witch's calf in the New York story, *J. A. F.-L.*, XVII (1914), 30 ff.

[195] Cf. *Autobiography of Brantley York*, p. 8; Scot, *Disc. of Witchcraft*, p. 8. Scot disbelieves the accounts of witches' "entering into men's houses, through chinks and little holes, where a flie can scarcely wring out" (p. 51).

[196] *Edn. cit.*, p. 114.

[197] See above, p. 220, n. 9.

[198] See, for example, Wright, *Narratives*, II, pp. 116, 176.

[199] See above, p. 223, n. 20.

maiden for some time as a servant, he married her. For several years the captive remained a dutiful and apparently contented wife, but on discovering one day that the keyhole had been unstopped, she escaped.[200] In a large number of cases witches are accused of entering houses to steal, as in the following negro story from Guilford County, North Carolina. A man who was losing molasses out of his cellar watched one night outside the house to catch the thieves. Three witches appeared, and each, saying "In an' out I go," dropped her garments and went into the cellar. The man kept the clothes, and presumably caught the witches.[201]

Much of the trouble that witches cause on their nocturnal rambles results from the exercise of powers which they possess in common with two much dreaded visitants of old—the incubus and the vampire: the former a lascivious demon close kin to the nightmare, who sometimes pressed the sleeper to death;[202] the latter a ghost or corpse (often of a suicide or murderer), who sucked the victim's blood till he died of exhaustion.[203] During the Dark and

---

[200] J. A. F.-L., XIV (1901), 40. Cf. vol. XIX, 243.

[201] J. A. F.-L., XXX (1917), 188.

[202] The tendency to attribute to witches characteristics of the succubus is also of long standing. See Scot, Disc. of Witchcraft, pp. 8, 81. The witches themselves were formerly accused of having sexual relations with an incubus or even with the devil (Cf. Scot, op. cit., p. 26 ff.). Scot asserts that in his day it was a universally accepted belief among authorities on witches that "the divell plaieth Succubus to the man, and carrieth from him the seed of generation, which he delivereth as Incubus to the woman, who manie times that waie is gotten with child; which will verie naturallie (they saie) become a witch, and such a one they affirme Merline was" (p. 56). Robin Goodfellow was also the son of an incubus and a mortal maid (Percy Soc., II, 6 ff.). On the incubus doctrine, see Cockayne, Leechdoms, I, xxxiii ff.

[203] The folk-lore of the Southern States still contains traces of the belief that the dead may return to injure the living. The negroes of the South Carolina coast sometimes drive a stake through a grave "to keep the spirits from haunting," and it is said that among the negroes of Norfolk, Virginia, the position of the door-knobs is changed after a death, "that the ghost may not find his way in" (F. D. Bergen, Animal and Plant Lore, p. 15). Successive deaths in the same family from consumption, poor sanitation, or other causes, are sometimes attributed to the work of vampires. The following is current among the Geechee negroes along the coasts of South Carolina and Georgia: "If you cannot raise your children, bury on its face the last one to die and those coming after will live" (So. Workman, XXXIV [1905], 634). See further J. A. F.-L., IV, (1891),

Middle Ages the incubus was much given to dishonoring mortal women in their sleep, and it is still known in southeastern Virginia that male witches sometimes visit their neighbors' wives at night. According to a sixteenth-century belief, the devil can assume the likeness of female witches and take their places in bed beside their husbands while the women themselves are absent on some diabolical errand. Vampire-like witches are still found in some parts of the United States. For example, in Clinton County, Pennsylvania, children who are hag-ridden at night are found in the morning "bruised on the chest and sore, with nipples bleeding from sucking." [204] Human beings are, of course, often "ridden" by witches, and it is recorded that a girl in one of the mountain districts of the South was "pressed to death" by a witch who came night after night in the form of a black cat and sat on her chest.[205]

253; Karl Knortz, *Der menschliche Körper*, p. 199; and p. 241, n. 60, of this paper. The theory that corpses do not always rest easy is, of course, strengthened by the numerous more or less authentic instances of bodies interred before the complete extinction of life. The following story, told by Col. Jas. G. Burr in an address delivered at Wilmington, North Carolina, in 1890, is said to be vouched for by persons of unimpeachable veracity. Two young gentlemen of Wilmington agreed that whichever died first should return to visit the other. Not long afterward one of them was killed by a fall from his horse. A few days after the funeral the survivor received a visit from his deceased friend. The latter revealed the fact that he had been buried alive, and added, "Open the coffin and you will see I am not lying in the position in which you placed me." The body was disinterred and was discovered to be lying on its face. (*James Sprunt Historical Monographs* (Univ. of N. C.), 4 [1904], 130 ff.). Dr. J. E. West, who was drowned while trying to ford the Tuckaseegee River at Bear Ford on March 19, 1881, appeared after a fortnight to the mother of one of his patients, told her where to find the body, and so impressed upon her the necessity of recovering the remains, that she dispatched a search-party in accordance with the directions given by the drowned man. The "corpse was found in the precise place she had pointed out to them." J. P. Arthur (*op. cit.*, p. 338), citing a personal letter from Colonel D. K. Collins. Most ghosts of today apparently have no purpose; this was one of those "robust and earnest ghosts of our ancestors" spoken of with such respect by Andrew Lang, whose admirable *Book of Dreams and Ghosts* should be consulted for a large collection of authentic cases.

[204] *J. A. F.-L.*, IV (1891), 324. Cf. *So. Workman*, XL, 587. For a seventeenth century case of a demoniacal creature which sucked a girl's blood through her nipples, see Fairfax, *Daemonologia*, edn. cit., p. 46.

[205] *J. A. F.-L.*, VII (1894), 114 f. About 1678 a girl in Lincolnshire, Eng., had a somewhat similar experience (*Sadduc. Triumph.*, p. 425). Compare

Sometimes the witch, by means of a magic bridle, transforms the sleeper into a horse, and then rides the animal until dawn. Next morning the bewitched person finds his toes and fingers covered with dirt, his limbs scratched, and his strength exhausted.[206] A story from southeastern Virginia tells of a man who, when he was about to be ridden by a witch, seized the bridle and forced it into the hag's mouth. The woman began to shift her shape rapidly in order to terrify her victim into relaxing his hold, but in the end was severely beaten. In Lincoln County, North Carolina, the witch's mount, instead of being a transformed human being, is an ordinary horse. The following day the animal is restive and fatigued, and the tangles in its mane, known as "witch-stirrups," are evidence of the use to which it has been put.[207]

the Maryland story, *J. A. F.-L.*, XIV, p. 39. Cats sometimes suck the breath of sleeping children (See above, p. 234).

[206] See the testimony of the Rev. Brantley York, *Autobiography*, p. 8. For more recent evidence, see *J. A. F.-L.*, XV (1902), 273 (Va.); II, pp. 32 (Pa.), 292 (N. H.); XXIV, 320 (Knott Co., Ky.). Professor E. C. Perrow, who was born in Virginia, writes that his grandfather, Joseph Graham, "knew a man who was ridden at night by witches. They bridled him and rode him to dances. They tied him outside where he could see the lights and hear the fiddles. He showed briars in his hand next morning from the briar patches through which he had been ridden." Cf. Notestein, *op. cit.*, 97 f. In a story from Lehigh Co., Pa., a witch transforms certain girls into snakes (*J. A. F.-L.*, II, 33). The following story was told in 1915 to Mr. Thomas Smith by Mrs. Peggy Perry, seventy-six years of age. A woman living in the "Breshy" district of North Carolina "got somethin' the matter with 'er, so's she went 'round bawlin' jist like a cow, and her little gal went 'round after her a-bawlin' jist like a calf. Ever'body said they wuz bewitched and I've heerd who they said bewitched 'em, but I'd rather not tell who it wuz, fer, you see, there's some o' his folks a-livin' 'round not fur off and they'd like as not git mad at me fer tellin' sich things. Well, the little gal finally died and they buried her in the yard right back o' the house, and some o' the neighbors, seein' as the pore woman didn't git any better—she wouldn't talk, but kep' bawlin' all the time like a cow—them neighbors went and sent fer old Keller, who wuz a witchdoctor. She got better right straight after old Keller come to see her. I don't know how he done, but he shore on-witched her." For a similar story from Kentucky, see Karl Knortz, *Zur amerikanischen Volkskunde*, Tübingen, 1905, p. 36.

[207] For examples, see *J. A. F.-L.*, VII (1894), 114 (Alleghany Mountains—white); IV, 324 (Pa.); XVII, 247 (S. C.-negro). Cf. F. D. Bergen, *Animal and Plant Lore*, p. 82. In County Clare, Ireland, fairies ride the farmhorses at night (*Folk-Lore*, XXII [1911], 449). During the Middle Ages fairies often rode on horseback. Cf. *Mod. Phil.*, XII (1915), 631, n. 2.

The witch's goal on her midnight rides is often an assembly like the one at which Tam O'Shanter assisted.[208] Among the mountain whites of the Alleghanies witches are powerless on Friday, but on that day can hear everything their enemies say against them.[209]

Of the numerous devices for keeping witches out of a house, many may be classified under a heading known to students of folk-lore as the "Impossible Task." In ancient Greek, Roman, and Oriental tradition malignant spirits who happened to fall under the power of mortals, were sometimes required to weave ropes of sand or perform similar feats.[210] Today the North Carolina mountaineer, when bedeviled by witches, hangs a sifter over the keyhole,[211] for he knews that the hag, before entering, will have to count all the meshes in the sifter, a computation she

---

[208] J. A. F.-L., XIII (1900), 210 (Scott Co., Tenn.); XIV, 39 (Md.-white). In former times witch meetings, or sabbaths, were accompanied by revolting and indecent rites (Cf. Scot, op. cit., p. 32 f.), and modern voodoo worshipers are charged with similar practices.

[209] J. A. F.-L., VII (1894), 11. In the sixteenth century it was believed that witches confess more readily on Friday (Scot, op. cit., p. 24). The sect of mediæval heretics known as the Eutychians were said to hold their orgies on Good Friday night (Scot, op. cit., p. 34). Though the bad reputation of Friday was doubtless enhanced by the tradition that Christ was crucified and that Adam and Eve ate the forbidden fruit on that day, the superstition of unlucky days extends far back into pagan times. See R. M. Lawrence, The Magic of the Horse-Shoe, p. 258 ff. Cf. Eliphas Lévi, The History of Magic, trans., A. E. Waite, London, 1913, p. 159; Chambers, Book of Days, I (1886), 42. Friday is still regarded as unlucky. "Friday is always either the fairest or the foulest day of the week" (Cumberland Mountains; E. B. Miles, op. cit., p. 107). It is bad luck to plant seeds on "Rotten" Saturday—the Saturday between Good Friday and Easter Sunday; seeds sowed on that day will rot in the ground. (Formerly current in parts of Lincoln County: Mr. Coon).

[210] Cf. J. A. F.-L., XII (1899), 69 f.; XVII, 126.

[211] Collectanea of the N. C. F.-L., Soc. For early charms and precautions against nightmare, see Scot, op. cit., p. 69 f. The writer has heard that in southeastern Virginia turning the key sidewise in the keyhole will prevent the witch from entering and that a flax-hackle placed on the breast of the sleeper with the teeth up will injure her when she tries to mount, and so keep her from riding. (Cf. J. A. F.-L., XXII [1909], 252). It would be interesting to know whether North Carolina witches, like the fairies of European folk-lore, can be placated by placing pails of water (or milk) in the kitchen at night, as is the case in Maryland (Cf. F. D. Bergen, Animal and Plant Lore, p. 15).

will be unable to complete before daylight arrives and forces her to leave.[212] In many sections, including the highlands of the South, a broom laid across the doorway is sufficient protection,[213] the true explanation of its value being that offered in Maryland: the witch cannot enter until she has counted all the straws of which the broom is made.[214] In Louisiana any one who refuses to step over a broom is a witch.[215] The mountain people of western North Carolina say that it is bad luck to step over a broom.[216] Another prescription recommends the sprinkling of mustard or other small seed in the four corners of the house; the hag, like the prince in the fairy tale, must pick up the seed one by one before she can be free.[217] The following negro version comes from Guilford County, North Carolina. " Ol' witch goin' from house to house. Too much work to do in one place. People throwed mustard-seed in her way. Had to pick up one by one befo' she lef'. 'Here I am, where shall I hide myself?' Says, 'I'll never get in a place like that again. Bes' way to carry gol' an' silver with me. I've done foun' out they can't do anything with the mustard-seed while I carry the gol' an' silver.' After she got her gol' an' silver, she did go all right. Didn't have to pick up the seed." [218]

Another group of charms against witchcraft apparently depends ultimately upon the awe with which primitive man regarded the newly discovered metal iron. Other-world beings have always

[212] In Alabama the sifter is placed under the doorstep; in Chestertown, Md., over the door (Bergen, *Animal and Plant Lore*, p. 16). Cf. *So. Workman*, XLI (1912), 246. In those Maryland prescriptions which direct that a fork be stuck through the sifter and that both be placed on the chest at night with the tines of the fork upwards, the function of the sifter has apparently been forgotten. Cf. *J. A. F.-L.*, v (1892), 110 f.; XII, 145. According to a negro tradition from Baltimore, the impossibility of the computation is due to the fact that a witch cannot count above five (*J. A. F.-L.*, XI, 76).

[213] *J. A. F.-L.*, VII (1894), 113 f. Cf. vol. IV, 126 (Ja.); XIV, 40 (Md.-white).

[214] *Ibid.*, XI (1898), 9.

[215] *Ibid.*, XVIII (1905), 230. Some Southern mountaineers say that any one who steps over a broom lying in a doorway is a witch. Cf. *J. A. F.-L.*, XII (1899), 132.

[216] *Ibid.*, XX (1907); 245.

[217] *So Workman*, XLI, 246.

[218] *J. A. F.-L.*, XXX (1917), 188.

shrunk from contact with iron. In a large number of folk-tales the beautiful fairy princess married to a mortal deserts her lover when he touches her, even accidentally, with a piece of metal, and the modern witch cannot enter a house on or above the door of which a horseshoe is nailed.[219] In the mountains of North Carolina it is lucky to find a horseshoe or a pin,[220] especially if the opening of the horseshoe or the point of the pin is directed toward the finder. Indeed, if you find a horseshoe and don't pick it up, you are liable to encounter misfortune.[221] The North Carolina housewife whose butter will not come may heat a horseshoe and apply it to the bottom of the churn, or, if the witches are particularly troublesome, she may even have to put the metal in the churn. If a red hot poker is inserted in the receptacle containing bewitched butter or soft soap, the witch is burned and the spell broken.[222] In Alabama whoever sleeps with a fork under his pillow need not fear being "ridden" at night.[223] Some twenty years ago in Georgia iron nails placed in a black bottle and buried under the door-step would keep off witches.[224]

Next to iron, the most popular metal now in use as a preventive against witchcraft is silver. Rev. Brantley York reports that in his youth witches in Randolph County, North Carolina, could be killed with a silver bullet. The Southern mountaineers of today believe that if an ox, fatally wounded with a hair-ball, is shot with a silver bullet, the witch will be injured.[225] In western Maryland shooting the hag's picture with a bullet made from a silver coin

---

[219] J. A. F.-L., XII (1899), 76 (Baltimore-negro). The value of the horseshoe is here explained on the same principle as that of the sifter; the witch, before entering, must travel over the path the horseshoe has taken. For other instances of the use of the horseshoe to prevent witchcraft, see J. A. F.-L., IV, 255 (N. H.), 323 (Pa.); V, 182 (Pa.). On the horseshoe in folk-lore, see J. A. F.-L., IX, 288 ff.; R. M. Lawrence, *The Magic of the Horse-Shoe*, Boston and New York, 1898, p. 1 ff.; Karl Knortz, *Amerikanischer Aberglaube der Gegenwart*, p. 31 ff.

[220] J. A. F.-L., XX (1907), 246.

[221] Collectanea of the N. C. F.-L. Soc. It is also bad luck to give away a pin in North Carolina.

[222] F. D. Bergen, *Animal and Plant Lore*, 21; J. A. F.-L., VII (1894) pp. 66 f., 115 (Alleghany Mountains).

[223] F. D. Bergen, op. cit., 16; J. A. F.-L., XII (1899), 261 (Ga.).

[224] J. A. F.-L., V (1892), 230.

[225] J. A. F.-L., VII (1894), 114.

is an effective means of retaliation.[226] In Georgia ghosts are killed with silver bullets, and the use of silver nails and screws in making a coffin will prevent the corpse from haunting the scenes of its earthly life.[227] Silver money carried in the shoe or worn on a string around the neck is a well-known charm against witch spells,[228] and even the wearing of a silver ring is alleged to have a certain protective value.[229] The following story, told by a hunter in Edgecombe County, North Carolina, illustrates the necessity of using silver bullets in shooting uncanny creatures.

Immediately after the Civil War there was a prevailing belief in Edgecombe County, that the low, boggy, heavily wooded district lying along Henrietta Creek was infested by witches. In spite of its bad reputation, however, the place was a famous hunting ground. One evening about sundown a hunter who had sat down to rest under a dead pine in the vicinity of the creek, was surprised to hear in the silence of the forest a mysterious tapping. Looking up he perceived near the top of the tree "what appeared to be a common woodpecker storing away food for the long, cold winter." After shooting at the bird without effect until his ammunition was exhausted, he cut a dime into small pieces, with which he loaded his gun and fired again. With a loud shriek the bird fell lifeless to the ground. "Ever since this occurrence," adds the narrator, "the people of Henrietta neighborhood believe that the only way to kill witches is to shoot them with silver."

Another story, from Lincoln County, is told by Mr. Coon. A witch man once assumed the shape of a turkey gobbler, and perched himself on the limb of the high tree beside the path of a famous hunter. Not recognizing the witch under this form of disguise, the man shot twenty-nine rounds at the bird. "Every time his gun would fire, the witch turkey would stand erect on his perch, shake himself, and sit down again. Disgusted with his bad marksmanship, the woodsman went his way. Not far from the scene of his discomfiture the hunter met a friend and related to him his

[226] J. A. F.-L., XIV (1901), 42. Cf. vol. IV, pp. 126, 324 (Pa.); F. D. Bergen, op. cit., 15 (Ala.).

[227] J. A. F.-L., VII (1894), 305.

[228] J. A. F.-L., XIV (1901), 179; XXIV, 320 (Knott Co., Ky.); IX, 226; F. D. Bergen, Animal and Plant Lore, 15. Cf. J. A. F.-L., XII, 228 f.

[229] J. A. F.-L., IX (1896), 226.

recent experience. His neighbor immediately pronounced the turkey a witch, and declared that it could be brought down only by a silver bullet. The hunter accordingly went home, and, after moulding a silver bullet, returned with his friend to the place where he had seen the witch. On their arrival, however, the bird flew away. Their suspicions were, nevertheless, confirmed by their encountering a few hundred yards off " a man who was famous all over the country as a witch of witches."

The value of silver in dealing with the powers of darkness is illustrated by a clipping from the Winston-Salem *Sentinel* for February 16, 1915, for which the writer is indebted to Mr. G. T. Stephenson:

" Jim Webster, a colored man who lives about six miles west of the city, believes in witches and wizards and hoodoos and all that sort of thing, and for forty years has carried a silver dollar in his mouth night and day, not to make his speech silvery but to keep away the hoodoo.[230] He keeps one dollar in his mouth until all the letters and figures are worn off, then he exchanges it for a new dollar. He says he is now wearing his fourth dollar. Jim thinks that as long as he carries that dollar in his mouth, witches and hoodoos have no power over him, so he works, eats and sleeps with it in his jaw. A large number of other colored people thinks (sic) the silver dollar in his mouth gives Jim some kind of hoodooistic powers, and they are rather shy of him." In a letter accompanying the article Mr. Stephenson writes: " I have talked with the negro and seen the dollar, and can vouch for the statements made in the clipping."

No account of the preventives against witchcraft would be even approximately complete without at least a word about salt. Reginald Scot was repeating an old tradition when in 1584 he wrote, " The divell loveth no salt in his meate," [231] for salt has always

---

[230] Some conjure-doctors begin the diagnosis of a case of suspected witchcraft by placing a piece of silver in the patient's mouth. If the silver turns black, the patient is suffering from the effects of witchcraft (*J. A. F.-L.*, IX [1896], 224). Cf. Karl Knortz, *Amerikanischer Aberglaube der Gegenwart*, 9. Professor Perrow received the following cure for witch spells from his grandfather: " Take a brand new silver dollar. Trim off shavings from it with a knife. Put these in a cup, pour hot water over them and drink the water."

[231] *Discoverie of Witchcraft*, 435. On the folk-lore of salt, see further

been used with great effect by the Christian church in putting to flight heathen divinities and other beings antagonistic to the people of God. In the sixteenth century judges presiding over witchcraft trials were urged to carry salt about their persons,[232] and today the mountaineers of the South know that salt worn in the shoe prevents "overlooking."[233] In western Maryland a witch is rendered powerless if salt is sprinkled under her chair,[234] and, as Harris's "Plantation Witch" shows, salt rubbed on a witch's skin after she has shed it, prevents a recurrence of the shape-shifting.[235] Most people know that when salt is spilled, bad luck is sure to result unless a few grains are at once thrown over the left shoulder.[236]

University of Chicago.

NOTE.—Further contributions will be gratefully received by the writer or by Professor Frank C. Brown, Secretary and Treasurer of the North Carolina Folk-Lore Society, Durham, North Carolina.

Grimm, Deut. Mythol., II, 876 f.; R. M. Lawrence, The Magic of the Horse-Shoe, p. 154 ff.

[232] Scot, op. cit., p. 23.

[233] J. A. F.-L., VII (1894), 114. Cf. F. D. Bergen, Current Superstitions, p. 82. In County Wexford, Ireland, peeled potatoes left on the hearth-stone for the fairies must not be salted (Mrs. S. C. Hall, Sketches of Irish Character, N. Y., 1845, p. 268). Cf. Sir Walter Scott, Letters on Demonology and Witchcraft, p. 124 f.

[234] J. A. F.-L., XIV (1901), 40.

[235] Cf. J. A. F.-L., V, (1892), 110 f. (Md.); IX, 129 f. (S. C.). In a confused negro story from Guilford County, North Carolina, a thievish witch who shed her skin in order to enter a store is prevented from returning by red pepper. As soon as daylight strikes her, she drops dead (J. A. F.-L., XXX, 187 f.). Professor Perrow heard from his grandfather a story of a witch who used to slip out of her skin at night and go abroad. "Her husband watched her and cured her by putting salt and pepper on her skin while she was away one night." In the seventeenth century rosemary was used in England as a preventive against witchcraft (Thomas Wright, Narratives, II, 137). A tradition from southeastern Virginia asserts that the plant was first brought to America by Grace Sherwood, the early eighteenth century witch.

[236] Cf. J. A. F.-L., XX (1907), 245 (N. C.).

CONTENTS OF VOLUME XIV, 1917

	PAGE
J. M. Steadman, Jr. The Origin of the Historical Present in English	1
Foreword	49
W. J. Lawrence. The Mystery of Lodowick Barry	52
Joseph Quincy Adams. The Conventual Buildings of Blackfriars, London, and the Playhouses Constructed Therein	64
Thornton Shirley Graves. "Playeng in the Darke" During the Elizabethan Period	88
Tucker Brooke. Hamlet's Third Soliloquy	117
John Matthews Manly. Cuts and Insertions in Shakespeare's Plays	123
Raymond Macdonald Alden. The Lyrical Conceit of the Elizabethans	130
Jefferson B. Fletcher. The Painter of the Poets	153
Charles G. Osgood. Spenser's Sapience	167
James Holly Hanford. The Dramatic Element in *Paradise Lost*	178
Edwin Greenlaw. "A Better Teacher than Aquinas"	196
Recent Literature	218
James Finch Royster. "I'll Not Trust the Printed Word,"	229
Samuel A. Tannenbaum. Hamlet Prepares for Action	237
C. A. Moore. The Return to Nature in English Poetry of the Eighteenth Century	243
Herbert Cushing Tolman. The Turfan Fragments on the Crucifixion	293
Clinton Walker Keyes. The Constitutional Position of the Roman Dictatorship	298
Elizabeth Breazeale. Polyptoton in the Hexameters of Ovid, Lucretius, and Vergil	306
George Howe. Polyptoton in Tibullus and Propertius	319

**University of Toronto
Library**

DO NOT
REMOVE
THE
CARD
FROM
THIS
POCKET

Acme Library Card Pocket
LOWE-MARTIN CO. LIMITED

CPSIA information can be obtained
at www.ICGtesting.com
Printed in the USA
BVHW050859131221
623913BV00002B/128